CHEVROLET 8.1L VORTEC/496 PERFORMANCE MANUAL

CHEVROLET 8.1L VORTEC/496 PERFORMANCE MANUAL

HOW TO MODIFY 8100 VORTEC TRUCK AND 496 CID MARINE ENGINES

LARRY HOFER & DON TAYLOR

Tucson, Arizona

Publishers
Howard Fisher
Helen Fisher

Publications Manager, Editor
Miriam Warren

Cover Design
Miriam Warren

Book Production and Illustrations
Doug Goewey

Interior Photography
Larry Hofer and Don Taylor, except where otherwise noted

California Bill's Automotive Handbooks,
Tucson 85719

Published 2020
Printed in USA

25 24 23 2 3 4 5 6

ISBN-13: 978-1-931128-41-4
ISBN-10: 1-931128-41-3

Library of Congress Cataloging-in-Publication Data is available.

This paper meets the requirements of ANSI/NISO Z39.48-1992 (Permanence of Paper).

Photo Credits

Front Cover

This gorgeous machine is a 725 hp, 572 CID PSI block with aluminum heads, custom accessory drives, water crossover, and stack fuel injections. All parts have been powder coated for a very clean look.

Back Cover

This is a completely assembled, 518 CID 8.1L, World block with aluminum heads and a 2.9 Whipple blower.

Table of Contents

Acknowledgments

This book was not created just by Don and me, but by many other people who have contributed time, information, and inspiration during the last forty years. For this we are both thankful.

One of the first persons to say thanks to is David Vizard. When I was in college, way back in 1974, I had the pleasure and fortune to meet David and the group of writers and authors in Tucson who were grouped around Bill Fisher and HP Books. At that time David was writing his Pinto and Small-Block Chevy books. He has graciously allowed Don and me to reference his *Chevy Big-Blocks: How to Build Max Performance on a Budget* book where applicable. His technical information in that book goes far beyond the scope of the 8.1L in how-to instruction. He was brilliant then and has only gotten better with time—like a fine wine. Thank you, David Vizard, for the years of education.

In the world of 496 CID 8.1L engines, the first who lent a hand was Merv Cray who discovered and brought me the first prototype 496-8.1 engine from Florida in 2000, just so I could see what it was. No one knew back then what the 8.1 was… now we would like them all to know. Thanks, Merv. After that, Ray and Mike Franks from Pro-Filer Performance Products were on the leading edge of producing an aluminum 496-8.1 head. What a long and hard learning curve that was. Their association with Reher Morrison Racing Engines led us to Darin Morgan who designed and engineered the wonderful intake and exhaust ports for the Raylar head. Next is John Fell, owner of Buddy Bar Casting, producer of the finest head castings for years, who supplied photos of how the heads are cast.

Greg Burkhart of GT Racing Heads has machined and produced perfect CNC finished cylinder heads for me for years. Yehoram Hofman of Hofman Design is the CAD computer engineer with all the GM 496-8.1 technical information, allowing me to create castings and digital information. Another important part in my learning of airflow was Steve Stanley of S D Engine-Flow-Rite, who worked with intake manifold and port design. Peter Lake of Aluma-Star casting taught me how to design and build tooling to cast intake manifold runners. In the early years of engine building and development on the dynamometer, was Britt Bostick of Ramona, California. Britt provided much of our technical information. Special thanks should go to Jason Thomas for letting me test so many parts on his 27' Fountain boat, to see what fell off, and Paul Murphy for his incredible knowledge of the performance boat world.

With regards to the development of the replacement engine blocks for the 496, first is Richard Maskin of Dart Machinery who worked with me to make their prototype 496-8.1 engine blocks a reality. Next is John Nachman, who has supplied me with unlimited information of, and for, the 496-8.1 engine. Last, but certainly not least, is Dick Boyer, CEO of World Products, makers of performance engine blocks and who has entered the arena of manufacturing a perfect copy of the 496-8.1 block. He has been most gracious.

To my favorite machine shop, Wholesale Automotive Machine Inc.'s owner, Jerry DeBerry, and his top-notch engine builder, Brent Lechleiter, who graciously supplied the photos of assembling and balancing one of my customer's engine, and who have built many engines for me without any failures—amazing!

To my mentor and co-author, Don Taylor, who booted me in the butt in 1982 and said, "Get going with life!" Yes, I did, and yes we did. In addition, a very special smile and thanks goes to his wife Ellen, for putting up with Don and me, and for the time we have taken away from her.

And another very special person, Barb Potts, my girlfriend of years. When I am late coming home from work, she is always there with a smile and something warm to eat, never complaining about the hours I work, and just letting me do my job. To her, I owe a huge debt of gratitude. Thank you, Barb.

Last, our most excellent and patient editor of California Bill's Automotive Handbooks, Howard Fisher, and his publications manager, Miriam Warren, whose help and coaching has made it easier to reach the goal of finishing this book. Howard has had many headaches editing our sorry spelling, grammar, and review of items we included and left out. Many thanks to you, Howard. Miriam was most helpful with her computer knowledge while we photographed our cover and back piece. Thank you, Miriam for all the work you have put into our book. We would still be there trying to get that cover photo done without your help.

There may be other people out there who should be on this list, and to you, we apologize, as you deserve much thanks and credit also.

—Larry Hofer and Don Taylor

About the Authors

Larry Hofer is the owner of The Corvette Shop and Raylar Engineering in San Diego, California. He has been involved in the performance automotive, truck, and marine industry for nearly forty years. Larry has written and contributed to several automotive publications, including *Vette* and *Hot Rod* magazines, and with Don Taylor, the *Paint and Body Handbook*, and *How to Rebuild Small-Block Mopar Engines*.

Don Taylor grew up in the auto business. He has written extensively on automotive upholstery, engine rebuilding, restoration, and paint and body work. Some of his titles include the *Automotive Upholstery Handbook*, *Custom Auto Interiors*, and *How to Rebuild Big-Block Mopar Engines*. Don lives in Concord, California.

Larry Hofer (left) and Don Taylor (right).

Introduction

In 2001, General Motors Corporation introduced the 496 CID 8.1L (liter) engine. This was to replace the 454 CID engine that powered so many boats, vehicles, and power plants for agricultural use. It made its debut in the 2001 Chevrolet Silverado and the GMC 2500HD and 3500 series heavy-duty pickup trucks. It made 340 hp at 4200 rpm, and 455 ft-lb of torque at 3200 rpm, improving the tow/haul capabilities of the new vehicles over the earlier 454 CID powered.

This newly designed engine was mated to a 4L80, four-speed automatic transmission, an all-new Series 1000 Allison five-speed automatic transmission, or a ZF six-speed manual transmission. In its marine application, the Vortec 8100 was available in two versions: the 375 hp and the 425 hp. These variations of engines made their way into trucks, boats, motor homes, and stationary power plants, and soon became the engine of choice for high-torque gasoline engines. GM was the sole manufacturer of this strong and durable engine for ten years. It was also the first GM big-block engine to pass the 300-hour, marine dock test.

About twenty-five percent of GM's 496 CID 8.1L engines were sold for marine use. Therefore, much of the testing on the Vortec 8100 was done using the marine market's more severe duty parameters. In one particular test, called the "Marine Dock" test, an engine is run at virtually wide-open throttle for 300 hours straight (60-minute cycle consisting of 55 minutes wide-open throttle followed by five minutes idle). According to GM, this testing is more severe than standard durability testing used for truck applications. They attempted to destroy the engine—but it survived!

When GM stopped producing this engine package in 2009, the market was open for other manufacturers to pick up the tooling and production of this engine. In 2010, Dart Machinery was the first to develop a similar block and put it into production for the marine and industrial markets. Following Dart's endeavor was Power Solutions International (PSI) in 2012. Their main interest was to manufacture complete replacements of the 496 CID 8.1L engines. They redesigned the heads and intake for their engines to their own specifications and requirements, and the short-block increased in displacement to 8.8L. The heads and intakes are not interchangeable with GM engines; however, the PSI block is completely interchangeable with GM Gen 7 block components. PSI's main interest is in complete engine packages for stationary generators, pumps, and heavy road chassis. Their engines start at 270 hp at 2600 rpm. From truck engines to turbocharged engines, they can develop 900 ft lb of torque at 2100 rpm, making them excellent engines for generators.

The latest to enter this engine production has been World Products, who already make many different types of GM engine blocks. They began developing this block in 2016. Their 8.1L replacement block is also an exact copy of the GM block, allowing components that fit on a GM GEN 7 block to fit on the World block.

In December 2009, GM suspended its production of the 496 CID 8.1L, leaving Dart, PSI, and World Products, as the sole manufacturers. However, to date, these engines are still collectively referred to as a General Motors' 496-8.1L product.

In this book, we are going to tell you everything that needs to be known about this product—except how to build one. For every use you can think of, there is a different way to build this engine. Instead, we will tell you about the block, oiling systems, cooling systems, cranks, rods and pistons, cylinder heads, intakes and fueling systems, cams and valve systems, computers, exhausts, and everything you need to know to help you select the right combination for your needs.

Now while we said we were not going to show you all the ways to create your dream engine, we have developed two chapters on engine building: head building and block assembly. These two processes are standard for each of the four manufacturer's engines. While the styles may change for advancing horsepower or torque, the mechanics are pretty much the same. This has been the good news—now for the bad.

These engines, all four brands, are not sold as complete assemblies to the average customer. Sad, but true. The reasons are twofold: 1) GM no longer manufactures this engine, and 2) the other three manufacturers only sell components, or in lots of 100s at a time! How do they get that many customers at one time? They sell only to groups with large fleets and quantities of vehicles such as UPS, FedEx, motor home manufacturers, and big boat builders. These are only a few of their well-known customers, but you can see why they are not interested in selling one engine at a time to an individual. So how can you get one of these big engines for your Mini Cooper? You'll have to search the junkyard or know someone like Larry Hofer. (Larry knows the guy at the bar, whose brother is on good terms with the guard at the back gate…) This is being facetious, but men like Larry are well-known to the manufacturers and have twenty to forty years in the business researching and developing product lines for these engines. As a thank you, they may slip one out to someone like Larry. Therefore, you may have to look around a bit for what you want—but it's out there.

We hope this book gives you the necessary information to find the right engine. If you are going to select an engine from a junkyard (by far your least expensive option) be sure to have it fully inspected to confirm it is in good condition. If you want a brand-new block, give Larry a call, whisper the secret password "800 hp" and I'm sure he will help you out!

1

Engine Development

The inception of the Gen 7, General Motors' big block, appears to be in or around 1994 or 1995. GM took the old technology of the Gen 4, 5, and 6 big-block platforms and adapted it to the emissions requirements projected for 1997.

Two different thermal cooling systems were tested to compare engine efficiencies. One cooling system used the reverse-flow coolant system, found in the 1992 to 1996 LT1. Cool water went into the front of the head through to the rear of the head, then down into the block, and back out the front. The other cooling system followed a more traditional water flow: water went into the front of the block, to the rear of the block, up into the rear of the heads, and back out the front of the head. There didn't appear to be any improvement in efficiency with this second, more complicated, reverse cooling system than in the original, so the reverse cooling system was dropped. One improvement learned from testing these two systems though, was that hot water could be kept out of the intake manifold by including a water crossover from both heads to an external thermostat housing. This addition of the external thermostat housing kept the intake air cooler because the intake manifold was not being heated by the water.

Another requirement for 1997 was that the engine be computer-controlled for emissions, as was available in the new LS1 small-block introduced in the 1997 Corvette. This control system included an X24 count crankshaft timing reluctor and an X1 camshaft reluctor.

Figure 1.01 This General Motors, 450 hp, 8.1L engine is being fitted for headers.

Several of the problems inherent in the original design of the big block were being addressed during this redesign as well. These included the ring seal, oil leakage, head gasket seal, assembly time, and component cost. Also, under review was the crankcase windage due to the crank fitting too tightly inside the block, which limited the stroke increase required for the 8.1L. The solution was to widen the lower portion of the 8.1L block to accommodate the larger diameter and mass of the 4.375-stroke crank.

The deficiencies listed above were in the initial 1963 big-block design and were greatly improved upon. The head gasket sealing issue was due to inadequate and uneven clamping pressure of the head gasket on the intake gasket side, caused by the location of intake ports on the number two and six cylinders on the even side, and numbers three and seven on the odd side. The cylinder head intake port location of the Gen 4, 5, and 6 heads precluded the production head from being configured with six head bolts per cylinder for all eight cylinders. There were ways to include the two extra head bolts per side to make the Gen 4, 5, and 6 heads effectively six head bolts per cylinder for all eight cylinders, thereby eliminating the blown head gasket problem. However, it was never included as a production solution to the head gasket problem. The port layout did not allow the two head bolts to be installed

Figure 1.02 Factory air-conditioning mounts on the 8.1L block. Details of other yellow markings will be discussed in future chapters.

Figure 1.03 Side view of the Dart block, showing the bigger water jackets and fuel pump boss that requires shaving for clearances of some accessories.

Figure 1.04 Among other things, this serpentine belt drives the Whipple Marine, 3.3 supercharger.

Figure 1.05 This carbureted, 540 hp, GM engine is fitted with aluminum heads and intake manifold.

Figure 1.06 One of the engines highlighted on the cover. This is a completely assembled, 518 CID 8.1L, World block with aluminum heads and a 2.9 Whipple blower.

without going through the ports. This problem was eliminated on the 496 8.1L by designing the heads with symmetrical port layouts that allow the two extra head bolts, per head, to be installed as a factory-installed improvement. The head gasket-sealing problem, when used with MLS head gaskets is now a non-issue.

Another problem was oil leakage. You could replace all the gaskets and stop the leaking—for a while—but in one or two years it would start leaking again. This was due to the old design of the gasket system used in the 1960s: gaskets made of cork and rubber, which begin to deteriorate the moment they hit air. The new, 496 8.1L has machined surfaces on the valve cover rails, pan gasket surface, and timing cover surface. The oil pan, timing cover, and valve covers are now entirely aluminum with machined surfaces and O-ring seals. Also, the top valve-cover gasket surface of the head was raised so the gasket was higher than the oil return level inside the valve cover—therefore it didn't need to sit in an oil bath. The Gen 5 and Gen 6 one-piece, rear main crankshaft-seal was included in changes to the Gen 7 which almost eliminated the oil leaks.

The complete engine was changed from SAE dimensions to the metric system, including all fasteners. The stock pistons are hypereutectic cast aluminum with very minimal expansion characteristics and a tight cylinder wall clearance, again for emissions. The ring package changed to thinner metric rings to reduce friction and improve ring seal. The top ring was moved up very close to the top of the piston, which reduced the area for unburned hydrocarbons (also for reducing emissions). This top ring land position resulted in a very thin top ring land on the cast piston and is the only weak area of the 496 CID 8.1L engine.

The new computer system could precisely control the ignition timing under all conditions and allowed the engine to run at the most efficient fuel to air ratio, producing the best economy and least amount of pollutants. Another feature of the computer was the ability to include

Figure 1.07 This gorgeous machine is a 725 hp, 572 CID PSI block with aluminum heads, custom accessory drives, water crossover, and stack fuel injections. All parts have been powder coated for a very clean look.

Figure 1.08 Bottom view of the prototype World block. It was bored to 4.500" with a 4.500" stroke crank that received aluminum heads and a 2.9 Whipple supercharger.

sequential port injection thus eliminating fuel being wetted on the intake ports and valves.

The heads' symmetrical intake ports also allowed the design of equal length, intake manifold port runners, which allowed the designers to target the range for maximum torque.

Why is the 496 CID 8.1L Better?

I'd like to enter some of my own thinking on this matter. It seems most mechanics and machinists don't want to work on these "upstarts," and I think maybe the term or idea of "upstarts" may be the problem. To begin with, let's look way back to the small-block Chevy engine.

In 1955 the first small block, a whopping, big, 265 CID, was introduced and it was a struggle getting its point across to the everyday mechanic and machinist. The old Ford flathead was the way to go racing and now, here comes this new upstart, the Chevy small block. Well, it took time, but guess what? Where is the Ford flathead now? It's in the history books and unless you're an old timer like me, you may have never heard of it! It took time but people began to recognize the strength of the small-block and embraced it whole-heartedly. It was a learning experience.

For years the small block was the top choice in racing engines and highly developed components were cheaply produced. The engine has been around for more than fifty years, now, and some changes were introduced along the way, namely fuel injection. Now, who would want something as complicated as fuel injection when we've had carburetion almost forever and it works just fine, thank you?!

When the advantages of fuel injection were finally realized, the industry accepted this system as the current, best technology. Fuel injection created big horsepower; the individual runners could be tuned; it allowed for better cam choices and parts were still dirt-cheap. Remember, there were fifty years of development and the particulars of this engine were understood to the smallest detail. Then, entered the LS series of the new small block.

Figure 1.09 Here is what's involved in building a computer loom for an 840 hp, 540 CID 8.1L that also received a modified 3.3 Whipple blower. Don't try this at home unless you really know what you are doing!

Figure 1.10 Another view of Jason Thomas's 27' Fountain that was our test boat for years. The engine here is a 588 CID Dart block producing 680 hp! This boat has been clocked at close to 100 mph.

Why in the world would GM want to change something that already works so well? If they wanted a lighter engine, they could have made the small standard block out of aluminum. Why change? Improved technology. Every facet of the old small block was analyzed and improved upon. After fifteen years of production, the LS has proven itself to be head and shoulders better than the traditional Chevy small block. It's taken awhile but everyone has embraced the LS-style engine, except for a few cases where the older small-block has an advantage. The point I'm making here, is that as much as engine shops and customers hate to change, the new technology made a better

Figures 1.11, 1.12, and 1.13 These three photos show the fronts of the 8.1L blocks. From top-to-bottom, this is the PSI block (see logo at the top). Next is the GM block; note the added ribbing at the bottom. Lastly, the World block with 8.1L cast into the top.

Figures 1.14 and 1.15 Here are two shots of a 1996, prototype General Motors, 8.1L engine that was in a truck for development studies. It still ran well when Larry received it in 2000. Note the reverse cooling system on the front and GM prototype numbers on the valve covers.

engine out of the General Motors small-block engine. The same goes for the new Gen 7, 496 CID 8.1L big-block platform.

The older 427 CID, 454 CID, 502 CID were, and still are, truly fine engines—well proven and durable. If you have one in your vehicle, there's little reason to change. There are worlds of aftermarket parts available to increase the power of these engines.

The Gen 7 is the result of GM taking the best improvements from the LS platform and incorporating these in the Gen 7 big block. The computer system is exactly the same as the early 1997–2004 LS computer system. The cylinder heads now use a symmetrical intake port configuration that eliminates the good port/bad port inherent in the Gen 4, 5, and 6 head. The intake manifold incorporates the symmetrical spacing of the intake ports and a long, equal length runner, to allow each cylinder to receive the same intake charge. The heads have a fast burn combustion chamber for good fuel burn. Because the intake ports in the head are symmetrical, GM inserted the two missing head bolts on the intake side of the head that was forever the head gasket problem of the Gen 4, 5, and 6. With the MLS head gaskets and eighteen head bolts per side, blown head gaskets are now a thing of the past.

The block received a lot of attention as well. First, the casting process was changed to a thin-wall casting process that was more precise than the sand castings used in the Gen 4, 5, and 6, and as a result, the blocks are now 50 lbs lighter. There are now five 4-bolt main caps to keep the crank in place rather than the normal two 2-bolt, and three 4-bolt caps in the earlier models.

The oil pan rail was widened for more crank clearance, and more room was added at the bottom of the cylinders to allow a new 4.500 crank to drop in with no grinding.

The oiling system was opened up and now includes ½" pipe ports for the oil cooler. The oil pan, timing cover, and valve covers are cast aluminum and use O-rings to eliminate oil leaks. The cam is a roller cam designed to reduce parasitic losses and allow for more aggressive cam profiles. Even the rocker arms were improved with an oil deflector tab to direct the oil into the pivot ball. This little magic was developed by Smokey Yunick for NASCAR racing. Another of Smokey's simple inventions was to remove the return water from the front of the intake manifold and redirect it out of the front of the cylinder heads. This kept the intake manifold dry and cooler.

Overall, GM did a wonderful job of creating a much improved big-block Gen 7, and they sold 100,000 engines a year for ten years, which means they're available in salvage yards at a reasonable price for hot rods, boats, and trucks.

One problem remains, however—metrics.

Yes, metrics. Machine shops say, "I can't read metrics and I don't have metric tools." They then add, "It has a computer and no carburetor! What to do, what to do?" Well, so are the LS series engines and the world has adjusted to them like ducks to water.

The Gen 7 engine package is a huge improvement in design and technology over the Gen 4, 5, and 6 big-block engines just like the LS was a huge improvement over the standard Chevy small-block. The Gen 7 will be around for years to come. Several large companies are gearing up to produce even bigger and better engine blocks to increase the displacement of the Gen 7, but time will tell.

The Gen 4, 5, and 6 engines are not going away, and neither is the Gen 7; it's the next bigger and better Chevy big block.

HIGHLIGHT: CLEARANCE PROBLEM-SOLVING

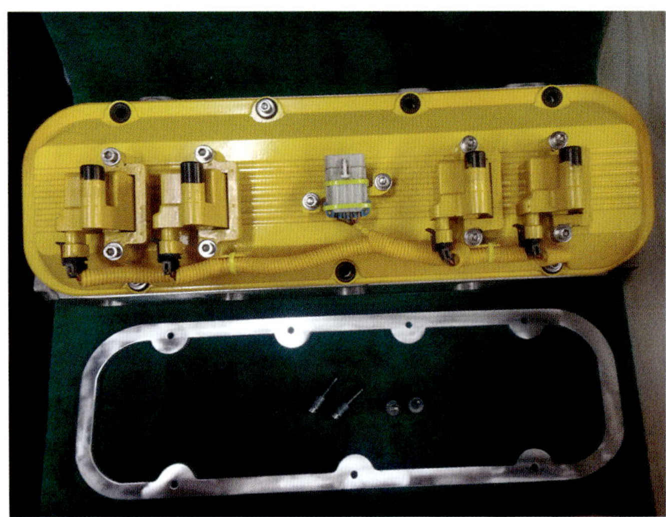

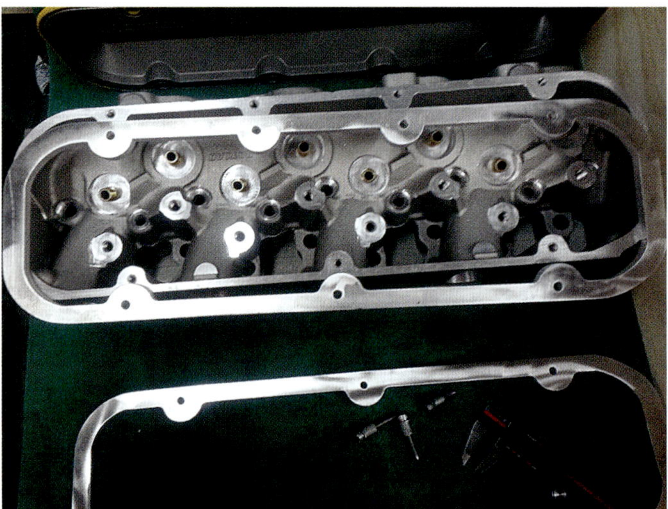

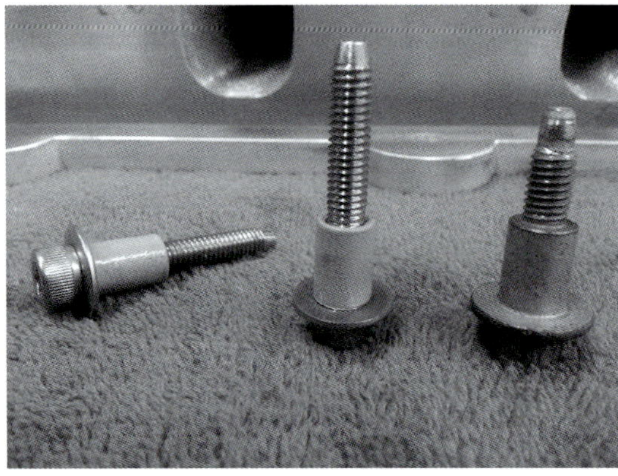

Figures 1.16, 1.17, 1.18 This is how Chris Lee solved his rocker arm to valve clearance problems, using a custom-designed spacer.

2

Big-Block Identification

In this chapter we will provide you with the necessary information to allow you to determine which block is which. It would be tough to discover you bought a used PSI block when you thought you were buying a General Motors piece. Those of you who need this information will be truly grateful, and those of you who know it already can spend some serious time looking for errors!

1996 General Motors, *Prototype*, 496 CID 8.1L

1. (Figure 2.01) Four head bolts per cylinder with ½" × 14" long head bolts into the main cap area of the block.
2. Cast aluminum oil pan, intake manifold, and timing gear cover. Similar to standard 8.1 engine but no cam sensor in cover.
3. Ends of the oil pan use wider radius than Gen 5 and Gen 6 as in the 2001 and up to 8.1L.
4. Block pan rails widened by 1" like the 2001 and up to 8.1L.
5. One-piece rear main oil seal like the Gen 5 and Gen 6 blocks.
6. (Figure 2.02) Cam sensor machined into the rear of the block. Sensor reads off a half-round reluctor on the oil pump drive.
7. X24 count crankshaft reluctor at the rear of the crankshaft like the 8.1L.
8. (Figure 2.03) Intakes have large, symmetrical oval intake ports.
9. Raised D-shaped exhaust ports like the 8.1L.
10. Block has the normal bore spacing as the Gen 4, 5, and 6 at 4.840".
11. Uses no distributor and runs the same computer system as the 1997–2004 Corvette and Camaro LS.
12. Coil near plug for high-energy spark.
13. Computer timing, ignition, and port fuel-injected with 27 lb injectors.
14. No mechanical fuel-pump location.
15. O-ring seals on pan, valve covers, and timing cover.

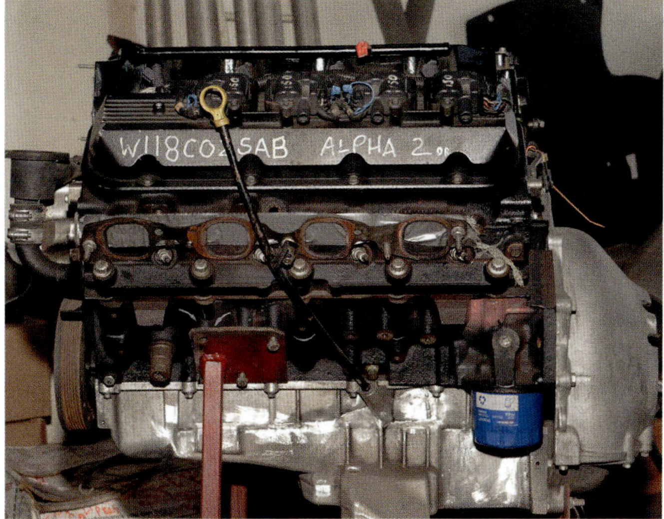

Figure 2.01 This beauty went into a 1999 C5 Corvette. Someone hand painted the GM prototype numbers on the valve covers. This engine has a custom-made intake manifold, oil pan, and Corvette bell housing. It was built in 2000.

Figure 2.02 These prototype heads have different-sized intake ports. As the engineering world moved along, ports were often opened up or reduced in an effort to increase or decrease horsepower and/or torque.

16. (Figures 2.04 and 2.05) Reversed (cooling) water flow in block and heads. With specially-designed reverse flow water pump, water flows into the front of the heads, to the rear of the heads, down into the back of the block, and returns out the front of the block similar to the 1992–1996 LT1 engine.
17. Callies' 4.375" stroke steel crankshaft.
18. Heavy duty big-block rods with 7⁄16" rod bolts.
19. Block has front and rear; 2-bolt main caps for the front and rear, and the middle three are 4-bolt main caps.
20. Uses a 454 CID windage tray.
21. Valve cover rails are raised to keep pooled oil off valve cover gasket seal.
22. Intake valves at 2.190", and exhaust valves of 1.720" with 3⁄8" stems.
23. Beehive valve springs.
24. Standard big block stamped rocker arms: 1.7 rocker ratio with no oil deflectors.
25. Standard big-block adjustable 7⁄16" rocker studs.
26. Valve covers same as 454/502 CID.
27. External block bolt holes similar to the 496 CID, but not an 8.1L.
28. Corner of block, cylinder #2, similar to the 8.1L.
29. Corner of block, cylinder #2, has location for the accessory bolt hole mounts.
30. Uses similar type Gen 5 and 6 hydraulic roller lifters.
31. Marine/industrial double-roller timing chain.

Figure 2.03 Here is a comparison view of the ports mentioned above in Figure 2.02. Notice their different size and shape.

Figure 2.05 Prototype 8.1L reverse cooling system. Note the location of the cooling tube crossover. Vapor vent tubes in the front and rear of the heads are reminiscent of the LT1 350 CID small-block engine.

Figure 2.04 On the left is shown a 2001 production 8.1L with the current cooling system. The right features a 1996 prototype 8.1L with a reverse cooling system. Note the different locations of the cross-over pipe.

2001 General Motors Production Block

1. Text "8.1L" cast between #3 and #5 cylinders, driver's side of block.
2. Bore spacing is 4.840".
3. Five 4-bolt main caps with 12 mm main cap bolts.
4. Main cap bolts have studs for windage tray.
5. Low volume oil pump with ¾" diameter oil pick up, which reduces parasitic power loss.
6. Heads use eighteen 10 mm × 1.5 mm bolts per head—two more than the Gen 4, 5, and 6.
7. Each head uses six head bolts on all four cylinders due to intake port configuration, eliminating head gasket problems.
8. Head bolts go through the block deck into the water jacket and must be sealed.
9. Oil pan widened for increased stroke clearance.
10. (Figure 2.06) Driver's side pan rail, by oil filter, uses ½" NPT threaded holes for oil cooler.
11. Block has increased windage and rotating assembly clearances.
12. Cast aluminum oil pan, intake manifold, valve covers, and timing cover sealed with O-rings.
13. Standard 427/502 CID big-block water pump configuration.
14. Intake manifolds incorporate MAP sensors, EVAP solenoid, internal PVC port, internal crankcase venting, EGR port (IAC for marine application), and external vacuum tap.
15. Uses ten 60- or 70- mm × 6 mm intake bolts.
16. Twenty-seven-pound fuel injectors, ¾" fuel rails.
17. Return fuel system used in 2001–2003 models. Non-return system in 2004–2009 blocks.
18. 2001–2003 with ⅜" fuel supply and ⁵⁄₁₆" fuel return with quick connect fuel lines. The 2004–2007 had ⅜" supply only.
19. Gen 5 and 6 hydraulic roller lifters and steel billet roller camshaft.

Figure 2.06 This shows the oil cooling system for an 8.1L marine engine. See where the cooler bolts to the block.

20. Lifters use "dog bone" lifter retainers.
21. Incorporates a camshaft valley tray for oil and intake manifold heat control.
22. Cast aluminum timing cover with O-ring seals.
23. Camshaft sensor moved to the timing cover.
24. Camshaft gear machined with grooves to work with camshaft sensors.
25. Marine/industrial has double-row timing chain.
26. Truck uses single-row timing chain.
27. Crank sensor is in rear of the block reading an X24 crankshaft reluctor.
28. Camshaft and crankshaft sensors produce a square wave signal for the computer.
29. The production engine used a cast iron crankshaft with 4.375" stroke. But there were a few 4.375" steel crankshafts used in the 2001 marine engine.
30. Steel connecting rods with 10 mm bolts.
31. Used cast 4.250" bore hypereutectic pistons with metric wrist pins.

Dart 8.1L Block (Purchased bare)

1. (Figure 2.07) Bore is 4.250" and can be bored to 4.600".
2. (Figure 2.08) Stroke comes at 4.375" and can be extended to 4.750".
3. Bore spacing is 4.840".
4. Block is extremely strong—60 lbs of extra metal.
5. (Figure 2.09) Outside of block matches Gen 4, 5, and 6 configurations, unlike the 8.1L.
6. Front corner of the deck at #2 cylinder is cut at a 45-degree angle. This corner cut of the boss removes the ability to mount the truck A/C bracket and marine fuel systems.
7. Unused fuel pump boss cast in core block which interferes with 8.1L OEM accessories. Can be machined off.
8. (Figure 2.10) Many external 8.1L bolt bosses are missing from the Dart block which are necessary to mount factory accessories.
9. Uses Gen 5 and 6 hydraulic rollers, dog bones, and spider retainers.
10. Does not have the oil cooler port locations on the oil pan rail to use stock 8.1L truck or marine oil cooler hook-ups. Must be made custom.
11. Gen 5 and 6 oil filter location on block.
12. (Figure 2.11) Oil pan rail widened to 8.1L pan width. Internal clearances are the same as Gen 4, 5, and 6.

Figure 2.08 H-beam rods and billet steel main caps in the Dart-M series block.

13. Tight crankcase clearance for 4.750" stroke crankshaft.
14. Block can be ordered with Siamese cylinder bores. Can be bored to 4.620".
15. Head deck is tapped for 7/16" × 14-thread head bolts.
16. (Figure 2.12) Splayed main caps—four-bolt, ½" × 13-thread bolts. Can build custom windage tray. If building custom tray, use a modified version of the Gen 4, 5, or 6 windage tray.
17. Uses Gen 7 crankshaft (one-piece rear main oil seal and timing reluctor).

Figure 2.07 Prototype of a Dart-M series, 8.1L set up for twin turbos in a marine installation. The large mass by the fuel pump boss limits accessory drives.

18. Rear main cap and front timing cover fit 8.1L GM oil pan.
19. Some early Dart prototypes used Gen 5 and 6 oil pans and front covers.
20. Deck is cast for blind head-bolt holes with Gen 4, 5, and 6 patterns.
21. Due to the 8.1L head-bolt layout, three head-bolt holes are drilled and tapped directly into the water jacket. Needs sealant.
22. Dart block is the only block with a Siamese water jacket.
23. To install a Dart block where there was an 8.1L, you will need to fabricate or modify many of the original components.
24. An excellent choice for a custom build.

Figure 2.09 This is a Dart prototype 496 block. It was originally a Gen 4 block. Note the widened oil pan rails and the Gen 4 oiling system. Also notice the extensions welded to the windage tray clampdowns. The windage tray will not interchange with a stock, 8.1L engine.

Figure 2.10 As you can see, there are no bolt holes for the stock marine oil cooler. It can be made to fit, but holes will need to be drilled and threaded.

Figure 2.12 Here is a close-up of one of the extensions of the windage tray legs made to fit this block.

Figure 2.11 Dart Big-M block with marine oil pan, aluminum heads, and marine exhaust manifolds.

PSI Block (Power Solutions International)

1. (Figure 2.13) Bore is 4.350". Can be bored to 4.400".
2. Stroke is 4.500". Can be increased to 4.750".
3. Bore spacing is 4.840".
4. Has all the original GM, 8.1L external bosses for accessory mounting.
5. Truck 2500 A/C bracket interference with block casting. A/C bracket must be modified.
6. Correct oil pan rails with ½", NPT threaded oil cooler connections in the correct location.
7. Correct aluminum timing gear cover and sensors.
8. Block has the correct #2 cylinder corner boss for the truck A/C and marine fuel pump attaching points.
9. Five main caps are 4-bolt mains. Bolts are ½" × 13 threads per inch.
10. Head bolts and most accessory bolts are 10 mm × 1.5 mm.
11. Head bolts extend into the water jacket and need sealant.
12. No windage tray from factory.
13. Can use ARP big-block main cap studs to install windage tray.
14. Main cap bolt spacing is different than GM, 8.1L.
15. Block has clearance for 4.500" stroke crankshaft. The 4.750" stroke crankshaft can be installed with mini-mum grinding.
16. PSI blocks come with under-piston oil squirters for piston cooling.
17. Uses GM roller lifters, dog bones, spider retainer, and roller camshaft.
18. Production engines have forged pistons but do not have eyebrows for high-lift camshaft clearance.
19. Uses steel I-beam rods and cap screws.
20. Comes with 4.500" stroke steel crankshaft and 4.350" diameter forged pistons.
21. Cast aluminum oil pan with O-ring seals.
22. Cast aluminum-timing cover with O-ring seals.
23. Uses 2004 and up camshaft sensor and camshaft gear.
24. Crankshafts can have either X24 or X58 count reluctors.
25. X24 count reluctors can be used with GM 0411 or 4896 computers, Mercury 555, Volvo MEFI 4 and 5, plus others.
26. X58 count reluctors can be used with the GM, E38, E40, E67, and many aftermarket computers.

Figure 2.13 Here is the PSI block for reference.

World Block

1. (Figure 2.14) Latest entry into the 8.1L arena; similar to the PSI block.
2. Block is purchased bare.
3. Bore is 4.250" and can be bored to 4.400". Stroke is 4.375" and can be extended to 4.750". Bore spacing is 4.840".
4. Heavy casting, semi-water core, good nickel content.
5. Correct 8.1L roller lifters, camshaft gear drive, and retainers.
6. Correct 8.1L oil pan rail width, crankcase area for windage tray and big-stroke crankshafts.
7. Oiling system is completely compatible with GM and PSI, 8.1L blocks.
8. All external mounting holes are metric and match the 8.1L.
9. Head deck is tapped for 10 mm × 1.5 mm like the GM and PSI blocks.
10. All five main bearing caps are four-bolt and use ½" × 13-thread bolts.

Figure 2.14 A World block.

Prototype Heads

1. Four head bolts per cylinder going all the way into the main cap area.
2. Symmetrical oval port arrangement. High-flowing ports.
3. Intake valve is 2.190", and exhaust valve is 1.720" with ⅜" valve stem diameter. Stock BB length.
4. Water crossover port is in front of the block, not in front of the head.
5. The heads use steam vent piping in the front and rear of the heads, similar to the 1992–1996 LT1 small-block.
6. Valve cover oil rail is raised to keep the oil puddle from seeping through the valve cover seal/gasket.
7. Combustion chamber is fast-burn design.
8. Has a single quench, heart-shaped, chamber.
9. Chamber volume is 114 cc.
10. Has raised D-shaped exhaust ports.
11. Uses standard big-block head exhaust-flange bolt pattern.
12. Weighs 78 lbs.
13. Casting is of the thin-wall, iron design.
14. Gen 4 and 5 ball trunnion, stamped rockers, 7⁄16" rocker studs.
15. 7⁄16" stud lock nuts.
16. Stamped guide plates for pushrods/rocker alignment.
17. Pushrods are ⅜".
18. Intake pushrod length is 8.180". Exhaust pushrod length is 9.130" long.
19. Iron heads have the combustion chamber size of 4.500" bore which is wider than the 4.250" cylinder bore. Therefore, as the intake air flows into the cylinder, it runs into a ⅛" shelf halfway around the bore. This shelf results in poor airflow.
20. No water is released from the front of the head as in the production 8.1L. Water flows back down into the front of the block and into the water pump for a reverse coolant flow. This is the reason for the vapor vent tube on the front and back of the cylinder head—to remove steam and air out at the highest point of the cylinder head, similar to the production models of 1992–1996 LT1, small-block, 350 CID engine. General Motors started this redesign of the 8.1L in the 1992–1996 era with the first block castings date-coded to 1996. Engines were completed for durability testing and installed in trucks.

Production Blocks (Iron Heads)

1. New, thin-wall castings, but they still weigh 78 lbs.
2. Eighteen 10 mm × 1.5 mm head bolts per head.
3. Stainless steel intake valves, 2.190" with $\frac{3}{8}$" stems.
4. Stainless steel exhaust valves, 1.720" with $\frac{3}{8}$" stems.
5. Beehive design valve springs have 90 psi spring-seat pressure spring rotators.
6. Rocker studs have 10 mm threads into the head and a $\frac{7}{16}$" diameter upper shaft with 8 mm upper threads, plus pivot ball, and lock nut.
7. Uses a non-adjustable valve train assembly.
8. Uses stamped rocker arms. This improved version uses an oil deflector on top to redirect oil sprayed from up through the pushrod hole and directly back onto the rocker pivot ball. This was also seen on Smokey Yunick's Trans Am small-block rockers that extended their service life.
9. There have been two manufacturers of the stamped pushrod guide plates: OPE and Radar—both are interchangeable.
10. Guide plates use 10 mm mounting holes and $\frac{3}{8}$" pushrods.
11. The 454/502 guide plates use $\frac{7}{16}$" mounting holes and are not interchangeable.
12. General Motors iron heads are either right side or left side and are not interchangeable due to the water outlet on the end of the heads.
13. Intake flange angle is 50.5 degrees off the deck surface as compared to the standard 45 degrees of the 427/502 CID.
14. Combustion chamber volume is 114 cc.
15. Heads are of a thin-wall casting design to minimize material used in manufacturing.
16. This type of casting makes the port walls thin, which limits the amount of porting.
17. Presents problems for the intake port on the short-side radius.
18. Exhaust ports are small but of a high-velocity design.
19. To improve the intake port, remove the bump next to the intake valve guide, smooth out the port castings, and consider taking this to a professional for a good valve job.
20. Remove minimal seat material for the valve job as any change in height shifts the location of the valve stem tip and effects the non-adjustable rocker height location.

HP3 Heads

1. General Motors intended to offer this head through GM performance outlets but wasn't successful.
2. Weight, 78 lbs.
3. CNC performance upgrade for 2003, 525 hp engine for GM performance. Innovation Marine and Champion Racing Heads were involved in development.
4. Heads were intended to make a 496 CID 8.1L into a 525 hp engine for GM performance sales and racing.
5. Installed larger valves and springs.
6. These heads are still used where class racing requires original iron heads, mainly for offshore marine racing.
7. Intake valves, 2.250" with $\frac{3}{8}$" stems
8. Exhaust valves, 1.800" with $\frac{3}{8}$" stems.
9. Dual valve spring at 160 lbs seat pressure.
10. Rotator eliminators removed and valve guides are cut down for increased lift.

Raylar Aluminum Heads

1. Weight is 38 lbs.
2. Designed by Darin Morgan of Reher Morrison Racing fame.
3. Originally cast by Pro-Filer Performance Products and machined at Roush Racing.
4. Intake valve, 2.190" × $\frac{11}{32}$" stainless steel.
5. Exhaust valve, 1.750" × $\frac{11}{32}$" stainless steel.
6. Combustion chamber volume 107 cc.
7. Heads went through several revisions ending up with complete CNC of the total head, including ports, combustion chambers, and valve seats.

Dart Iron Heads

1. Weight is 75 lbs.
2. Configuration similar to Raylar Aluminum heads made for the industrial and marine engine replacement market.
3. These heads are sold bare.
4. Intake valve, 2.190" (or larger), 11⁄32" valve stems
5. Exhaust valve 1.750" (or larger), 11⁄32" valve stem.
6. Iron guides are stock. Stock 496 CID 8.1L valves will not drop in place.
7. You must use 11⁄32" valves or machine guides to 3⁄8" diameter.
8. Stud uses 7⁄16" threads into the head and 7⁄16" stud diameter like the 454/502 CID rocker studs.
9. Difficult to get poly lock adjusters under stock 496 CID 8.1L valve covers with these studs.
10. Bolt pattern of 496 CID 8.1L valve cover is different than the 427/502 CID stock covers.
11. Taller GM covers are not interchangeable.
12. Stock 8.1L valve covers mount the coil near the plug ignition system. This can be modified but would require custom work.

Figure 2.15 Custom made, 1⁄8" thick aluminum spacers used to fit between the intake manifold and the heads.

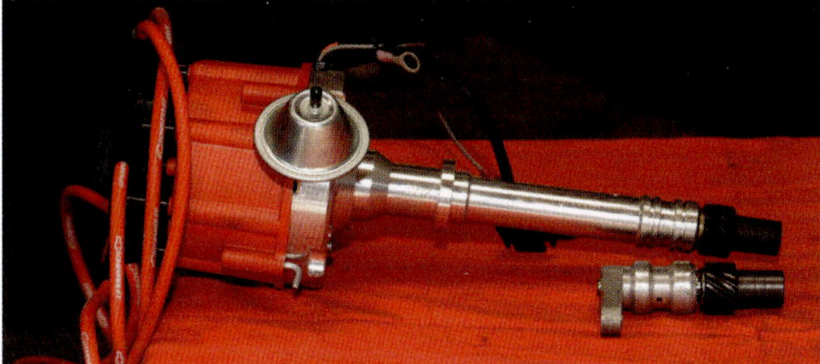

Figure 2.16 Compare the short oil pump drive used with the fuel injection system and the GM distributor used when incorporated with a Dart intake manifold.

Figure 2.17 Comparison of the two different types of valve covers. The black one is stock, and the silver is a custom, aftermarket product for the 8.1L.

Figure 2.18 Small-block rollers on the left, stock 8.1L lifter retainers with big-block rollers on the right. Note the orientation of the rollers at the bottom.

3

Cranks, Rods, and Pistons

You're driving comfortably along the highway as you pull up behind a Mercedes Benz. Though you're not thinking about it, you notice on the trunk lid edge the initials "AMG 63"—now what's that all about? Well, I'll tell you.

In 1967 two young men set up a little shop in Germany where they began doing speed work on Mercedes Benz race cars. Hans Werner Aufrecht, born in the town of Grossaspach, and his friend Erhardt Melcher began a thriving business building high-performance engines. What to call it?

(A)ufrecht
(M)elcher
(G)rossaspach

And what was that 63 you saw after the AMG? Well, it actually means 6.3 liters, or the displacement size of the block in cubic liters. Pretty nifty! So why do we bring that up here?

In 1967 Aufrecht and Melcher proposed the necessity of a blueprinted and balanced engine for the highest performance. As history moved forward their two-man shop became a full-fledged department of Mercedes Benz, manufacturing full-size racing type cars for the public. Now, my friends, let's see what this is all about in American cars.

Blueprinting

All of us know what a blueprint is, but let's take a closer look at its definition as it applies to this chapter. Blueprinting an engine is the process of creating a drawing to show the fitting or machined dimensions of the individual components of an engine to produce the best fitment and clearances to accomplish a specific objective. Every piece of machinery has a set of blueprints drawn up that define the minimum and maximum allowable dimensions at which a component will work without being damaged. The minimum clearance between mating components will allow a component to last as long as possible with an increase in parasitic drag. The maximum allowed clearances will allow the components to move as freely as possible and this, in turn, removes internal parasitic drag. In an engine, this results in more useable horsepower at the crankshaft. Blueprinting an engine is the process of determining what and how to assemble an engine with clearances that will allow the engine to have the least amount of internal friction and still not destroy itself.

Balancing

For an engine to run smoothly it's important that all similar reciprocating and rotating internal components be of matching weight. To accomplish this, all pistons, rings, and wrist pins are matched in weight. The piston, connecting rod, big ends and small ends, are matched in weight, and these values are inserted into a formula to produce another weight-value number. This weight value is attached to the crankshaft rod journals (called Bob weights) to simulate the piston and rod weight. Then, as the crankshaft is spun at a constant speed, any out-of-balance or vibrational condition in the crankshaft is removed by either adding or removing weight from the counterweights. Determining the correct weight will produce the smoothest possible rotating assembly. Check our sidebar for all the details on this operation, but remember it is very difficult to get a rotating assembly perfectly smooth at all crankshaft speeds.

Bore Sizes

We can now turn our attention to the various bore sizes. General Motors began building its 496 CID 8.1L engines with a standard bore size of 4.250". These can be bored safely to .030" to 4.280". You can push it to .060", to 4.310" but the cylinder bores become thin. Be sure you have your block sonic tested if you should decide to bore your engine this far out.

PSI engines begin with a block bored to 4.350" and can be bored safely to 4.400". Larry has never bored a PSI block beyond these specs but believes it can be done. The cylinder wall, as stated above, would be thin. If you're going for high horsepower, think twice before over-boring these engines.

World Products builds two blocks. The first is a water block for stock replacement that has water between the cylinder jackets. It can be bored like the GM block to 4.280" and we have seen them bored to 4.310". Larry bored one to 4.500" and after sonic testing found the walls on the non-thrust side to be .060", which is very thin. The second World Products block is the Siamese block. It could be bored to 4.600". This block, however, is still in prototype stage.

Finally, Dart makes two blocks—the first being a 4.250" engine, boreable to 4.280" safely and we have seen them bored to 4.310". The second is the Siamese block, which, at this time, can be bored to 4.600"!

Crankshafts

Figure 3.01 View of a stock, 8.1L cast-iron crank manufactured by General Motors. Normally there would be a Woodruff key cut into the crank, but GM decided it would be less expensive to drill this hole and press in a dowel pin to line up the lower timing gear. Unfortunately, this is where cracks develop, and the front of the crank can break off!

Figure 3.02 This crankshaft was cast and can be identified by the very thin parting line of the casting. Note the cast-in knife-edge on the counterweights to reduce windage. You will also notice the extra metal that was added to the rod journal end to equal the strength of a forged steel crankshaft.

Figure 3.03 This is a good shot of the cast crank part number. It also shows the extra metal and heavy counterweights needed for the cast iron crank.

Figure 3.04 Note how trim this forged steel crank is at the ends of the rod journals. It doesn't need the extra metal here as in the cast crank.

Figure 3.05 This is the signature mark of all cast cranks—the fine line of the casting tool.

Figure 3.06 Now, compare this forged crank with the wide flashing marks and you can readily see the difference between the forged and cast parts. You can also easily see the difference in textures between the two.

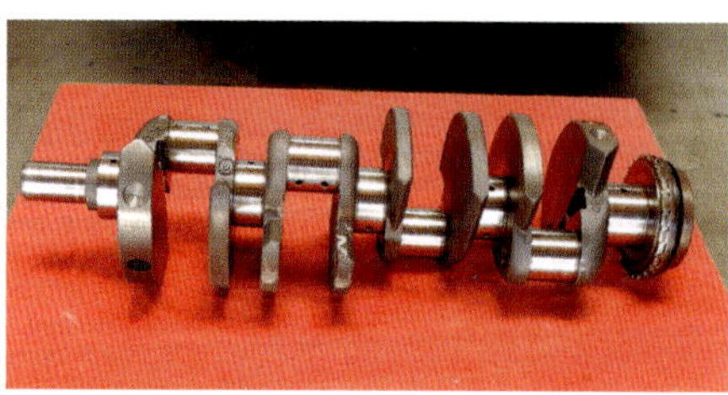

Figure 3.07 A standard 8.1L cast crankshaft.

Figure 3.08 This is the X24 count timing reluctor on the rear of the crank.

Figure 3.09 This is where the timing reluctor will fit at the end of the crankshaft.

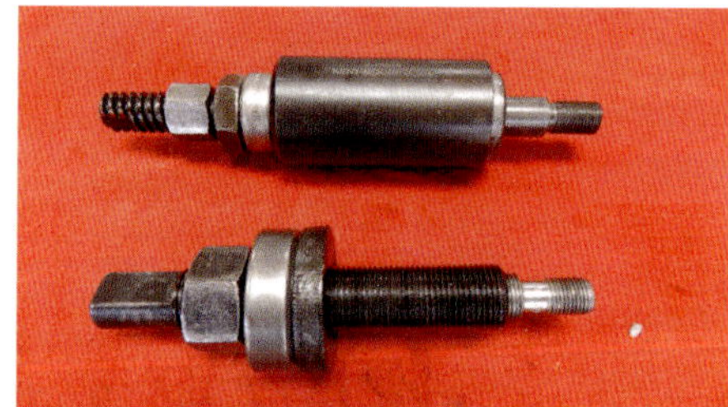

Figure 3.10 Here are the correct tools for installing the crankshaft dampener. The top one is a GM tool for the 8.1L crank with a 16 mm thread. The lower one is for the ½" thread used on the standard GM big-block and aftermarket steel cranks.

Figure 3.11 On the table sit four of the most commonly used crankshaft dampeners. From left to right is a 4500 and up industrial dampener. Next, we have a marine dampener typical of Mercury Marine. Third, is the standard 2500 and 3500 8.1L truck dampener. Lastly. the one on the right is a standard 396–427 CID neutral balance dampener that can be used to make special accessory drives.

Reluctor

All General Motors, Gen 7, 496 CID 8.1L crankshafts, since the introduction of the Gen 7, require timing reluctors. These are press-fitted on the rear of the crankshaft in front of the rear main seal. These reluctors are used to indicate to the computer where the crank is in relation to top dead center on the number one piston for ignition timing. These timing reluctors are what set this crankshaft apart from the Gen 5 and Gen 6 one-piece rear main seal crankshafts that have no provision for these timing reluctors. Below are the stock stroke sizes of most of the available Gen 7 crankshafts.

Cast cranks (stock)	4.375" stroke	2001–2009 GM
Steel cranks (stock)	4.375" stroke	2001–2002 GM (very rare)
Steel cranks (PSI)	4.500" stroke	2010 to current
Steel cranks (Raylar)	4.500" stroke	2004 to current
Steel cranks (Raylar)	4.750" stroke	Custom

Grain Structure

This is the metallurgical description of how the atoms of steel or aluminum are aligned and interconnected inside the material. For a cast grain structure, the easiest way I can think of to describe this is by example. Fill a cup with sand, add some glue or casting resin to the mix, and let it dry. This will form a very hard substance that is strong but brittle. It is only as strong as the bonding agent holding it together. There is no additional strength in the sand. The strength is only in the filler material. If it were to be hit with a hammer, it would shatter into many smaller parts. Cast aluminum pistons are the same way. The 8.1L came stock with cast pistons and they work very well up to the strength designed into the pistons, about 550–600 hp. Then they will break.

In a forging, there is a pattern in the arrangement of the atoms inside of the material, be it either aluminum or steel, which causes the internal structure to be connected one atom to the other. A good example of this is wood. All the fibers are inter-connected to one another and can be bent or beat upon, but the base material will not break. You can cut and shape it into things, but it will not shatter like a casting. This is why a forged engine part, either aluminum or steel, is stronger, will handle more horsepower, and is preferred when making a performance engine. The reason that cast aluminum and iron components are used in a production engine is mainly cost. Cast parts are "good enough" for the low power levels of production engines.

Pistons

The 8.1 comes stock with a hypereutectic cast piston. It works very well in the stock truck configuration. It's set up with .0015" piston-to-wall clearance. The top ring land is .200" thick. The first and second rings are .078" (2 mm) and the oil control ring is .158" (4 mm). The wrist pin is 1.040" diameter.

From 2001 to 2003 the wrist pin was press-fitted into the connecting rod. From 2004 and up, the wrist pin was a floating pin design and used wire ring clips to retain the wrist pin in the piston. This was done to reduce piston noise when the engine was cold.

The wrist pin centerline is 1.370" down from the top of the piston with the 4.375" stroke crank and stock connecting rods. They also have a very minimal valve notch on top of the piston for the intake valve clearance. This small

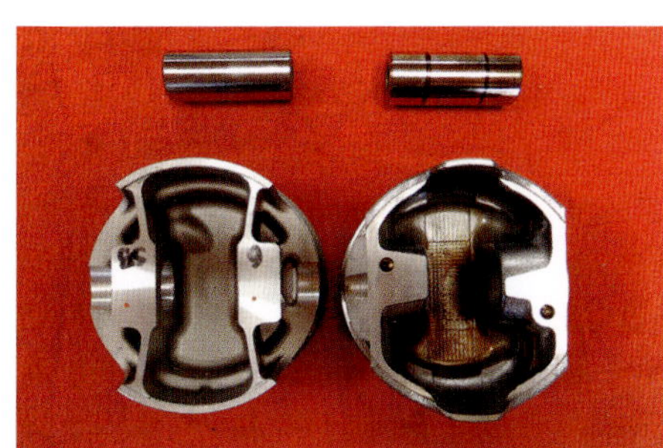

Figure 3.12 This is the underside of a forged piston at left and a cast piston on the right. You can tell the difference because the forged piston is smooth and looks polished, while the piston on the right contains lines from the casting process.

Figure 3.13 On the top is a stock, cast piston, with a very shallow valve relief. The bottom piston is a forged unit with a deeper and larger valve relief cut into the top.

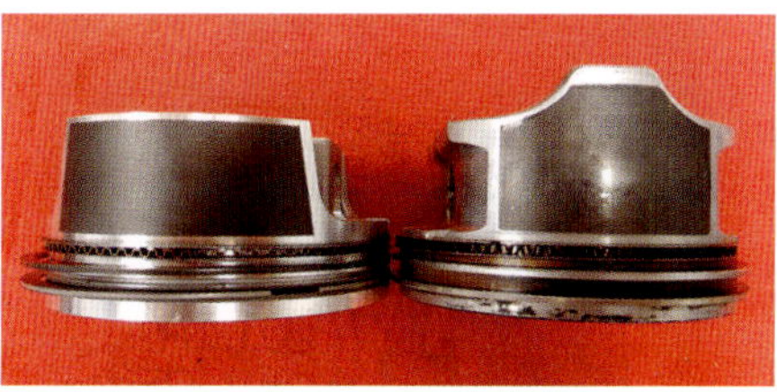

Figure 3.14 The piston on the left is a stroker piston with the shortened skirt. On the right is a stock, cast piston.

Figure 3.15 An example of a damaged piston.

Figure 3.16 Another classic image of a damaged piston.

BALANCING

All Photos Courtesy of Brent Lechleiter, Wholesale Automotive Machine, Inc., Jerry DeBerry, Owner

Larry and I decided the best way to get these pictures was to send the camera to Brent Lechleiter of Wholesale Automotive Machine, Inc. and ask him to photograph the entire balancing process for addition to this book. Our thanks go out to him for the fine work he did. Thanks, Brent, you did a swell job!

Figure S3.01 This strange looking construction is the crankshaft sitting in a balancing machine. Attached to the rod journals are individual balancing weights. The round fixtures are called bob weights. The bob weights are added to duplicate the weights of the rods and pistons. Weight is added or removed from the crankshaft counterweights until there is no vibration.

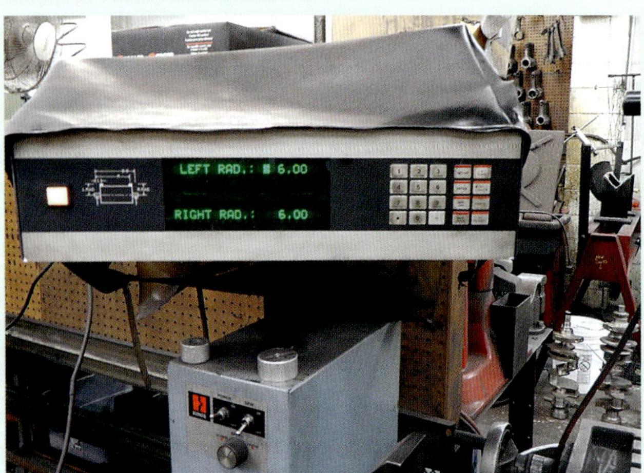

Figure S3.02 Sitting off to the side is the computer readout for this balancing project. When both numbers read .0000 kg the crank is in neutral balance.

Figure S3.03 This belt polisher is used to remove extremely small amounts of metal from the crankshaft journals. This is how the bearing clearances are opened up to the desired specifications.

Figure S3.04 Each rod will have both ends weighed and matched. Here, the big end is being weighed.

Figure S3.05 Now, the big end of the rod is being measured and resized to match the rod bearing bore size.

BALANCING (continued)

Figure S3.06 This is a good view of what is actually happening. Note that the scale is weighing in the metric system.

Figure S3.07 Each piston must weigh the same, with no variance exceeding .0000 kg.

Figure S3.08 Both pistons and rods have been balanced and are now ready to go together.

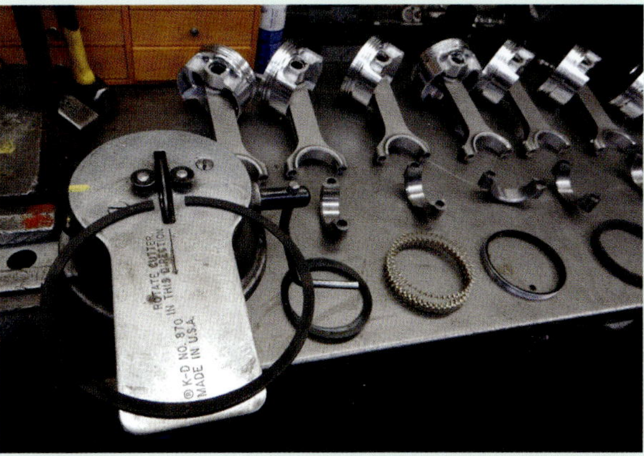

Figure S3.09 With the rods and pistons assembled, the piston rings are being filed to fit for each cylinder.

Figure S3.10 Brent has now assembled the pistons, rings, and rods. To finish the process the bearing dimensions must be confirmed. Note the micrometer in the lower right corner measuring the bearing half.

Figure S3.11 Sometimes when you ask for help, things get confused. Here the gang is boring a Ford block—woops! It's a great picture of the boring machine, however.

BALANCING (continued)

Figure S3.12 Here's what we wanted: our 8.1L is being honed.

Figure S3.13 This portion of the block has been aligned and bored, the bearings are in, and now Brent is using a dial gauge micrometer to make sure all bores are the same diameter within the prescribed tolerances.

Figure S3.14 The crank now sits in the block. Notice the reluctor on the end of the crank, inside the block. What's that long rod sticking out? It's the tool used to install the rear crankshaft oil seal.

Figure S3.15 Our block and crank have been put back together and the main caps bolted to spec. The big wrench at the top is to turn the crank to be sure everything is free.

Figure S3.16 Now our engine is finished, and oil testing has begun. Here, Brent is checking the rear main seal for leaks.

BALANCING (continued)

Figure S3.17 This is a very interesting machine. The crankshaft is attached to an electric motor that turns the engine at 400 rpm. The amperage of the electric motor can be measured, this in turn indicates whether the engine is tight or free. At the same time the oil is pumped into the oil filter bosses to lube the bearings and inspect for leaks while the engine is spinning. This allows Brent to document and measure the load on the electric motor. Also, the leakage from the bearings can be monitored. If you look carefully you can see three tiny streams of oil squirting out of the front main lifter galleys.

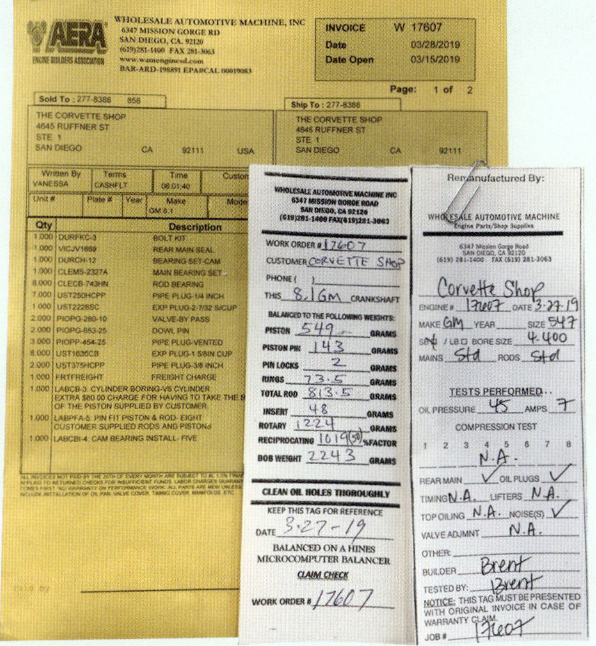

WHOLESALE AUTOMOTIVE MACHINE, INC
6347 MISSION GORGE RD
SAN DIEGO, CA. 92120
(619)281-1400 FAX 281-3063
www.wamenginesd.com
BAR-ARD-198891 EPA#CAL 00019083

AERA ENGINE BUILDERS ASSOCIATION

INVOICE W 17607
Date 03/28/2019
Date Open 03/15/2019

Page: 1 of 2

Sold To : 277-8388 856
THE CORVETTE SHOP
4645 RUFFNER ST
STE 1
SAN DIEGO CA 92111 USA

Ship To : 277-8388
THE CORVETTE SHOP
4645 RUFFNER ST
STE 1
SAN DIEGO CA 92111

Written By	Terms	Time
VANESSA	CASHFLT	08:01:40

Unit #	Plate #	Year	Make
			GM 8.1

Qty		Description
1.000	DURFKC-3	BOLT KIT
1.000	VICJV1669	REAR MAIN SEAL
1.000	DURCH-12	BEARING SET-CAM
1.000	CLEMS-2327A	MAIN BEARING SET
8.000	CLECB-743HN	ROD BEARING
7.000	UST250HCPP	PIPE PLUG-1/4 INCH
1.000	UST2228SC	EXP PLUG-2-7/32 S/CUP
2.000	PIOPG-280-10	VALVE-BY PASS
2.000	PIOPG-653-25	DOWL PIN
3.000	PIOPP-454-25	PIPE PLUG-VENTED
8.000	UST1635CB	EXP PLUG-1 5/8IN CUP
2.000	UST375HCPP	PIPE PLUG-3/8 INCH
1.000	FRTFREIGHT	FREIGHT CHARGE
1.000	LABCB-3: CYLINDER BORING-V8 CYLINDER EXTRA $80.00 CHARGE FOR HAVING TO TAKE THE B OF THE PISTON SUPPLIED BY CUSTOMER	
1.000	LABPFA-5: PIN FIT PISTON & ROD- EIGHT CUSTOMER SUPPLIED RODS AND PISTONs	
1.000	LABCBI-4: CAM BEARING INSTALL- FIVE	

WHOLESALE AUTOMOTIVE MACHINE INC
6347 MISSION GORGE ROAD
SAN DIEGO, CA 92120
(619)281-1400 FAX(619)281-3063

WORK ORDER # 17607
CUSTOMER CORVETTE SHOP
PHONE ( )
THIS 8.1GM CRANKSHAFT
BALANCED TO THE FOLLOWING WEIGHTS:
PISTON 549 GRAMS
PISTON PIN 143 GRAMS
PIN LOCKS 2 GRAMS
RINGS 73.5 GRAMS
TOTAL ROD 813.5 GRAMS
INSERT 48 GRAMS
ROTARY 1224 GRAMS
RECIPROCATING 1019 (50) %FACTOR
BOB WEIGHT 2243 GRAMS
CLEAN OIL HOLES THOROUGHLY
KEEP THIS TAG FOR REFERENCE
DATE 3-27-19
BALANCED ON A HINES MICROCOMPUTER BALANCER
CLAIM CHECK
WORK ORDER # 17607

Remanufactured By:
WHOLESALE AUTOMOTIVE MACHINE
Engine Parts/Shop Supplies
6347 Mission Gorge Road
SAN DIEGO, CA 92120
(619) 281-1400 FAX (619) 281-3063
Corvette Shop
ENGINE # 17607 DATE 3-27-19
MAKE GM YEAR SIZE 547
STD / LB ☐ BORE SIZE 4.400
MAINS Std RODS Std
TESTS PERFORMED
OIL PRESSURE 45 AMPS 7
COMPRESSION TEST
1 2 3 4 5 6 7 8
N.A.
REAR MAIN ✓ OIL PLUGS ✓
TIMING N.A. LIFTERS N.A.
TOP OILING N.A. NOISE(S) ✓
VALVE ADJMNT N.A.
OTHER:
BUILDER Brent
TESTED BY: Brent
NOTICE: THIS TAG MUST BE PRESENTED WITH ORIGINAL INVOICE IN CASE OF WARRANTY CLAIM.
JOB # 17607

Figure S3.18 This is the type of build sheet you should get when everything is finished. It records all the weights and values.

valve notch mentioned ealier limits maximum valve lift before valve contact with the piston causes engine damage.

When a high-performance engine is being built, and cost is not the final determination of the components used, forged pistons are usually included in the list of parts for the build. They offer many major advantages such as increased strength, choices in bore diameters, compression ratios, valve notches, ring package dimensions, wrist pin size and locations, and thicker top ring lands.

With all of these piston options you can account for crankshaft stroke increases, desired compression ratios, and many other factors to optimize the engine for a particular application. There are many piston suppliers for these types of custom pistons. It is best to talk to the supplier of choice and fill out a specification sheet for your application.

Connecting Rods

Here are a few interesting facts that Larry has provided us. I think they're worth going over.

The 8.1L came with a steel I-beam connecting rod. It uses either a pressed pin at the top of the rod for 2001 to 2003, or a floating pin from 2004 to current.

The center-to-center length of this rod is 6.705", pin diameter is 1.040", and the rod journal size is 2.200". They use a 10-mm rod bolt. GM recommends the replacement of these

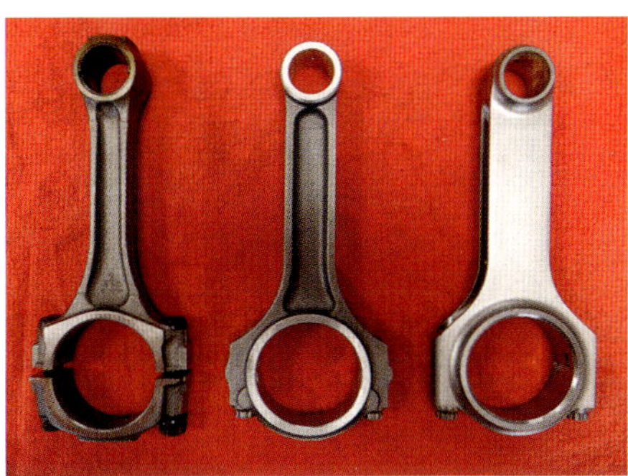

Figure 3.17 Here we show a stock 8.1L rod on the left, an aftermarket I-beam in the middle that has been profiled on the sides, and an H-beam rod that is completely machined on all sides.

Figure 3.18 This is a side view of the three connecting rods as seen in Figure 3.17. Here you can see the machine work that was done on the sides of the H-beam rod (bottom rod).

bolts after every disassembly. These rods generally do well in stock applications but are not the rod of choice if you want to build a high-performance engine—or if you want to go racing—due to the rod bolt design and limited strength.

Another problem with the stock rod and bolt configuration, is that when it's used with a longer stroke crank, such as the 4.500" or the 4.750", the rod and bolts hit the engine block as the crank rotates. This can be overcome with grinding, but it's better to use the correct rod in the first place.

Aftermarket Connecting Rods

Today there are many suppliers that carry outstanding connecting rods at a reasonable price. They are produced with better steel, machining, and therefore are stronger and lighter weight. They also come in a variety of better shapes, such as I-beam or H-beam sections, different lengths, and use better cap screw rod bolts. By profiling the rod and using cap screw rod bolts, there will be less chance of the rod interfering with the block when used with the longer stroke crankshaft.

There are also other metals used in connecting rods such as titanium and aluminum. Titanium rods would be wonderful, due to their lightweight and less rotating mass, but they're out of most people's price range. Aluminum rods have a place in top fuel-racing engines because of the compressibility of the rod. It saves the rod bearings when you're pounding them with 800 hp or more. However, aluminum connecting rods don't have the durability required for an endurance engine and therefore should not be used in vehicles of that type.

4

Cylinder Head Assembly

We come to the section of the book where we must determine what kind of heads we'll use on this beauty: aluminum or iron. So, let's look at some facts. When you compare the stock iron head to the aftermarket aluminum head, the iron head works well for the performance level for which it was designed, specifically 350 to 400 hp-level truck or marine engines. The aluminum head was designed for increased airflow and higher performance, but at an added price. In addition to cost, we must consider weight. The weight of the iron head is 78 lbs each compared to 36 lbs each for the aluminum heads. This means 156 lbs for the iron heads versus 72 lbs for the aluminum heads; which is a very large difference. In addition to being lighter weight, the aluminum head breathes better than the iron head. To build a high-performance engine we will need this lighter, better-breathing head to achieve what we're looking for.

Larry's company, Raylar Engineering builds these aluminum heads and is the only worldwide producer. With more than 30 years' experience as an aftermarket engineer, designer, and producer, it is worth your time to take a serious look at this product. For further information visit www.raylarengineering.com.

(See Figures 4.01 and 4.02.) Figure 4.01 shows a cross section of an aluminum head that has been cut through the valve center. Figure 4.02 is the same cross section of an iron head. Observe the two greatest areas affecting airflow: 1) there is a large obstruction beneath the valve guide where the valve passes through into the port, and 2) is on the floor of the port, where the floor makes a radical 60-degree downturn into the intake valve seat. At high speeds, air can't make this radical change in direction, which is a *serious* problem. In the iron head, air simply will not pass through these obstructions smoothly.

Figures 4.01 and 4.02 On the left is a cut through the aluminum head, while the right shows the same cut through an iron head. Refer to these when we describe how to make the iron head breathe easier.

Air likes to travel in one direction only, and that is straight. It doesn't like to change directions. When air hits an object and is forced in a different direction, swirls are created at that bending point. If you watch swiftly flowing water hit a rock, you can see these swirls. Each bend and resulting swirl significantly subtract from the airflow. In the iron head, there are several bends, limiting the maximum available airflow. In the aluminum head, bumps and direction changes have been removed. Therefore, air flows smoothly through the intake port, and makes a smooth turn into the valve seat area without the swirling and restrictions of the iron head. We'll address this further in Chapter 10, Big-Block Assembly, but for now assume about a forty to fifty percent increase in airflow using the aluminum heads instead of the iron heads.

The aluminum heads work well because they were designed specifically for the 496 CID engine bore size and intake system. No compromises were made in the design.

Matching Chamber to Bore Size

As mentioned earlier, the aluminum heads were designed to fit the GM 8.1L engine with a bore size of 4.250". With a 4.400 and larger bore block, the combustion chamber needs to be blended to enhance airflow into the bore. Therefore, we must make the head combustion chamber the same size as the bore. The following process is not needed if you have a bore diameter of 4.250" to 4.31".

The first step will be to transfer a witness mark from the block to the head. There are two ways to do this.

First, if the block is bare, bolt the head to the block. Then, from underneath, using a sharp scribe, reach up to the head through the bore and scribe a line around the bore, into the head. The second method is a little trickier—more often than not, the block will already be built, and you'll need to work from the top down.

Larry begins by lightly brushing white or red grease around the outside rim of the bore (both sides) (Figure 4.03). He then sets the head down onto the engine block and bolts it down. Because the head is so flat (machined to be that way) there is little room for error. He then removes the bolts, lifts the head, turns it over so the grease marks are facing up, and sets it on the bench (Figure 4.04). With the head-deck surface facing up, we can see a perfect outline of the bore. Now we can see how much of the chamber needs to be removed.

You should now have everything ready to scribe a line in the head to cut to. Larry likes to set the head in his lap while he makes this line (Figure 4.05). Very carefully scribe a line along the inside of the grease. Take your time and don't rush—enjoy a good cup of coffee while you do this! When all of the lines have been scribed, wipe off the grease, get a roll of ½" diameter masking tape and mask along each line you've made. Yeah, it looks pretty crummy and I'll give you another suggestion for it. First, remember Larry's been doing this since he was a boy and there's little chance of him making a mistake. Now, the suggestion: go to a paint and body shop and buy a roll of ⅛" masking tape. This is often called pin-stripping tape. Use this first to outline your incision. It's very flexible and will make a nice smooth line, then finish with ½". tape. Before cutting, place a valve in its seat to prevent damaging the valve seats.

Using a die grinder (Figure 4.06) with an aluminum fluted carbide cutter, *carefully* begin cutting the edge back (Figures 4.07 and 4.08). After both edges of the chamber are cut back to the line, use a 60-grit sanding roll (Figure 4.09) and smooth down the cutter ridges. The final step will be to

Figure 4.03 Larry creates witness marks by applying white grease around the tops of the bore.

Figure 4.04 Clamping the head to the block transfers the grease to the head to show how much you'll need to cut away.

Figure 4.06 Die grinder with an aluminum fluted carbide cutter.

Figure 4.05 Larry can scribe a line anywhere. Here, he sits in his chair, scribing a line without tape.

Figures 4.07 and 4.08 With the lines taped, Larry begins to cut back the edges.

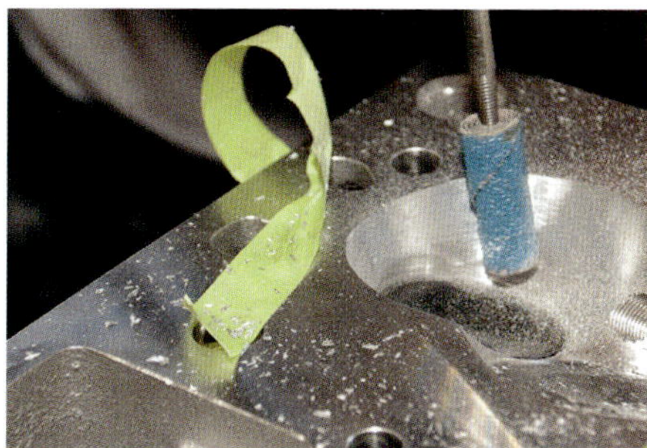

Figure 4.09 This is the 60-grit sanding roll. It removes the ridges created by the grinding and prepares the surface for using the sanding flapper.

Figure 4.12 These "head feet" are a terrific part to have on hand if you're going to be assembling more than one head.

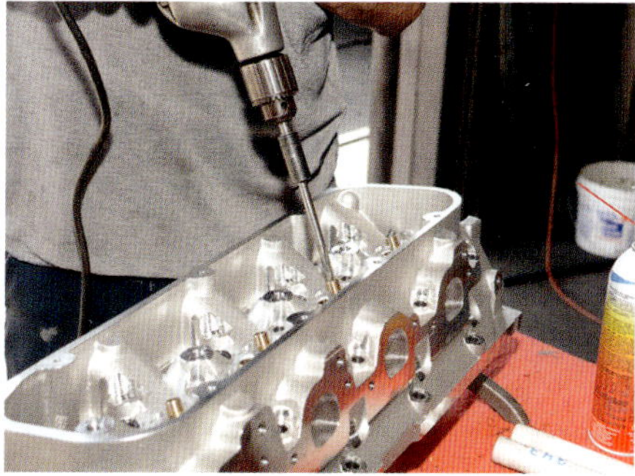

Figure 4.13 The bronze valve guides are installed by the machinist who does the CNC work on the head.

Figure 4.10 Finish off the job by polishing each chamber with the sanding flapper.

Figure 4.14 Oiling all the new parts is one of the most important steps of doing the job correctly. A couple of drops will do the trick. Be sure it's spread evenly through the guides by sliding a lightly oiled valve up and down through it.

Figure 4.11 If you're copying these directions, this is what a head looks like after being expanded by ¼". All we need to do is blow the grindings off and the job is done.

polish each chamber with a 120-grit flapper-sanding wheel (Figure 4.10). Once you have completed these three steps correctly, the eight chambers will match identically to the block and we're ready for the next step (Figure 4.11).

Assembling the Heads

Flip the head over and, if you have them, insert the head feet as shown (Figure 4.12). These iron feet allow you to pass a tool through the head without running into the table below and are available through Summit Racing Equipment or JEGS High Performance Parts. If you don't have a pair of these, or don't wish to buy them, a 2×4", 4" long will work as well.

Turn the head(s) face-up so the bronze valve guides are visible. These valve guides were installed as part of the CNC manufacturing process. The first step is to ream the guides (Figure 4.13). Reaming the valve guides will standardize the inside diameter and determine the working clearance of the valve. Insert the reamer into the guide and spin downward. *Be absolutely sure your reamer is the same size as the diameter of the valve stem plus the clearance for oil you want. A mistake here can ruin the head!* Remember: ⅜" stem for a stock valve and ¹¹⁄₃₂" for the aluminum head valve. Slide the reamer through the guide two or three times to ensure the inside of the valve guide is polished. When all the valve guides have been reamed, you're ready to install the valves.

Lay out all the valves for the first head (Figure 4.14) and place a drop or two of oil into the valve guide. Unwrap

Figure 4.15 Larry spreads a drop or two of oil on the valve stem and pushes the valve up and down while turning it back and forth. This ensures a good oil film on the valve stem and guide.

your valve and rub a bit of oil onto the shaft. Drop the valve into the guide, slide it up and down, give it a couple of twists to be sure everything is oiled, and proceed to the next one (Figure 4.15). You don't want any scratches in the valve guides. If there are any catches or hang-ups, it's probably on the groove where the valve keepers lock in. If needed, take a fine file and do a bit of smoothing around this groove, which should fix the problem. In the event it should bind somewhere in the middle, you have a bent valve, and will need to replace the entire valve. All the valves should feel the same as you slide them through the guides. Flip the head over so you can begin work on the other side (Figure 4.16).

The next step is to install the spring seats and shims (Figure 4.17). Spring seats and shims keep the springs centered and from grinding into the aluminum head and allow the spring to rotate with minimal friction. They also keep the retainers from binding on the top of the spring and being eaten away. We'll work on the valve stem seals next.

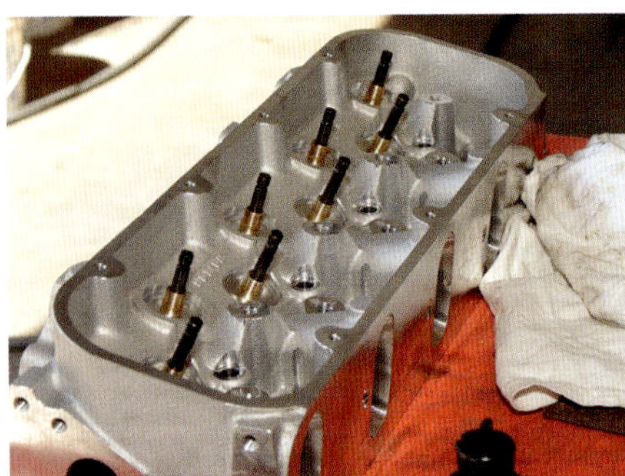

Figure 4.16 All the valves and valve guides have been oiled. With the head flipped over, the valves stay in place and don't fall back.

Figure 4.17 Begin by dropping the spring seats and shims over the valve guides.

Valve Stem Seals, Springs, and Retainers

Valve stem seals are flexible and contain a spring in the center to prevent oil from backing up around the valve stems. Because they take so much wear, they give out a little earlier than the rest of the engine. If your original engine was burning oil, failing valve stem seals could be one of the reasons. *Never try to save money by using old ones!* Now, let's turn our attention to the valve springs (Figure 4.18).

Engines of yesteryear did not have to wind up so fast and used more conservative camshaft profiles than today's high-lift, fast-ramp rate, roller lifter cams that are so common today. Only a single spring was needed. With modern big-block engines, we use an inner and outer double spring with a flat dampener. Yes, there are all kinds of ovate beehive valve springs that save mass, or remove internal friction, or have progressive spring rates, or are better for high rpm. The double spring has more weight, friction, heat, and other drawbacks, but when one spring fails the remaining spring holds the valve away from the piston. If a single valve spring fails, the valve will contact the piston and catastrophic damage will result. To avoid the risk of failure with a single spring, all Raylar heads receive the traditional dual spring with dampeners.

Figure 4.18 Valve stem seals in place.

There's one more part to look at —valve spring retainers. Valve spring retainers sit on top of the spring. The retainer performs two functions: retain the spring and clamp the two valve stem locks in place. These next steps require you to work slowly and carefully.

Larry uses a pneumatic valve spring compressor (Figure 4.19) as he runs a professional shop. If you do not have this instrument (as you only use it for this one operation) go to your nearest tool rental store and rent a hand-operated compressor. It will have a big lever on the top to compress the spring and works quite satisfactorily. When the spring is collapsed to where you can see the valve-keeper groove, install the two keepers (Figure 4.20). Finally, we install the OEM pushrod guide plates (Figure 4.21). The pushrod guide plates align the rocker-arm tip over the valve stem by holding the pushrod in the correct place. They are retained by rocker studs which are torqued to 55 ft-lbs.

At this point we have assembled the head to the point where it's ready for installation on the block, (Figure 4.22). We'll deal with the remaining parts at that time (See Chapter 10).

Figures 4.19 and 4.20 Larry uses a pneumatic valve spring compressor to compress the spring down allowing him to put the two keepers into the grooves on the valve stem.

Figure 4.21 Pushrod guide plates align the pushrod tip over the valve stem by holding the pushrod in the correct place.

Figure 4.22 Here, all valves have been installed, seats, shims, and springs, then capped off with new retainers. The big valve allows the intake air in and the small valve lets the exhaust out.

CASTING

All photos courtesy John Fell

Larry and I thought John Fell's sidebar on head casting might be interesting to the artist in you—so you artistic ones sit back and enjoy.

Sand casting is a process wherein there are several "permanent toolings" that are used to produce aluminum castings that can be used over and over again. There are two of these—the drag, or bottom tooling and the cope, or top tooling. The drag, which is the bottom tooling portion, produces the sand core for deck surface for the cylinder head and combustion chamber. The cope, which is the top tooling portion, produces the sand core that is the top of the head, rocker stands, and valve cover surface.

Assembled inside these two permanent tooling sand cores are: a brown sand core for the intake runners, (specially made); a brown sand core for the exhaust runners (specially made); and a white sand core, (again, specially made) that makes the cavity for water inside the head. The top and bottom sand cores are made from a material that can be used over and over. The rest of the cores must be pre-made for each head. All parts that are made of sand contain a plasticizing material that partially burns up/crystalizes allowing the technician to remove the sand. Note the white sand core for the cooling system: it melts at a higher temperature so that the exterior sand core does not collapse into the interior cores.

The cope is a bit like the cover for everything, although it must be precisely aligned, glued and sealed, and then clamped tightly to the drag. Remember: metal expands when it is heated.

Figure S4.01 This is the drag portion of the casting box being filled with sand to take the shape of the combustion chamber side of the cylinder head.

Figure S4.02 Finishing off the fill of sand in the drag box.

CASTING (continued)

Figure S4.03 Remove the cured sand from the box and this is what you have. Note the two long channels running along the top and bottom. These are alignment bars ensuring that all parts stay in precise alignments.

Figure S4.04 The technician now installs the water core. This white sand core melts at a different rate preventing the sand from the drag falling into the water core.

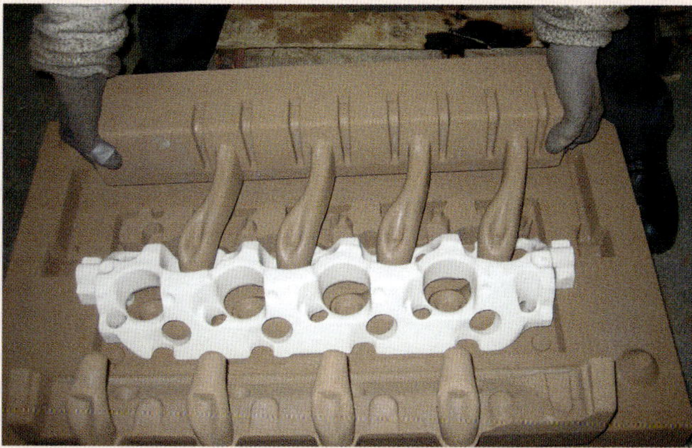

Figure S4.05 The technician now installs the intake core, assembled earlier, and the exhaust core waits for its installation. Both cores have locking grooves to ensure close fit tolerances.

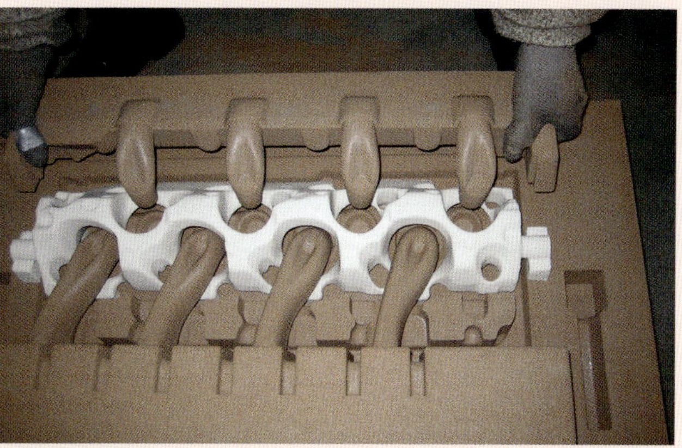

Figure S4.06 Now we can see the exhaust core being installed.

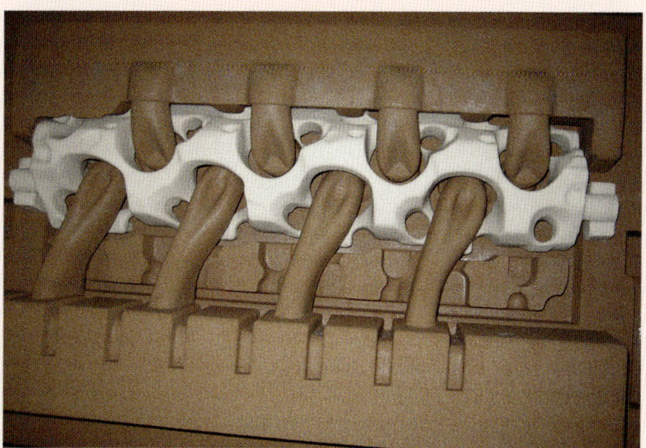

Figure S4.07 All three cores are in place.

Figure S4.08 Our technician sets a wooden block in place before the sand is poured. This leaves a giant hole in the center of the mold. As the molten aluminum is poured into the mold, impurities rise to the top and center. After the sand is removed this big projection is sawn off and thrown into the remelt pile.

CASTING (continued)

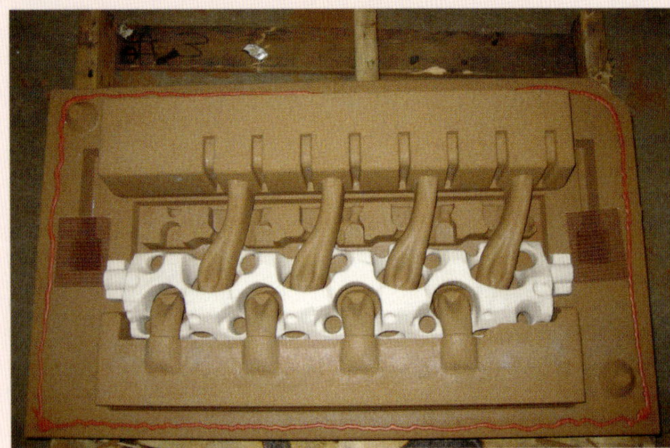

Figure S4.09 Sealing the bottom core (drag) to the top core (cope). Note the tapered cones in the top left corner and the bottom right corner. These are the alignment cones.

Figure S4.10 Dropping the cope onto the drag.

Figure S4.11 Everything is together now and we're ready for the pour.

Figure S4.12 Molten aluminum is poured into the core until it flows out the center where we saw the big wooden block being inserted (See Figure S04.08).

Figure S4.13 This is a finished casting for a single cylinder head. As you can see, this is a very time-consuming and labor-intensive operation to produce a quality casting

5

Cams and Valve Trains

Way back in the '50's every motorhead wanted a 1941 or '46 to '48 Ford Coupe. Why were these such desirable cars? Well, it was relatively inexpensive, had an easy-to-work-on flathead V8, and didn't cost an arm and a leg. World War II was over, and people were developing race parts as fast as they could. But in every young man's mind, the first thing to do was pull the cam, take it to the machine shop, and have the lobes reground just a touch so the valve would stay open just a bit longer. This improved the horsepower, therefore the speed, and now you could go drag racing! (Well, perhaps just a few other touches first.)

As I write this, I remember what that cam grinding cost: $30.00. That was about half a week's wages back then—well, for me that was what I netted. Today, you would buy a whole new cam for around $500.00—still, a half a week's wages. Time doesn't change things so much.

Figure 5.01 This is a front view of the World block with the stepped nose of the roller cam. It also has a long 8 mm bolt in the front to add leverage so as not to scrape the cam bearings.

Camshafts

The 496 CID 8.1L engine has benefitted from all the previous years of development. Roller cams were developed for the small-block, 350 CID Corvette engine beginning in 1986 through 1996. From 1997 until today, it has been run in the LS engine, the Gen 5, 454 CID truck engine (starting in 1996 and staying in place until 2000). The Gen 6, 454 CID, 502 CID, and the 572 CID began using the new roller cam in 1999 which is still in use today.

Roller lifters have several benefits: they last much longer than a flat-tappet lifter, and they have reduced parasitic friction due to the roller (which adds up to free horsepower). You can add a much faster ramp rate with a roller cam profile and open and close the valves faster. This means that for a specific valve opening duration, there will be more valve area open under the valve lift curve and higher volumetric efficiency for each cylinder. This higher efficiency produces more horsepower but also keeps the same idle characteristics of a smaller cam.

The cam profile for the 8.1L differs from a standard big-block cam with a different firing order (1, 8, 7, 2, 6, 5, 4, 3) and was never designed for use with carburetion. The timing specs were designed to capture the high-pressure air pulse in a very long intake runner. This simulates a very slight supercharging effect if the rpm, runner length, and cam timing can be optimized for a particular engine. This "Ram Tuning" effect was first discovered in 1958 by a group of Chrysler engineers nicknamed, "The Ram Chargers."

To this effect the lobe separation of the stock cam is very long—119 degrees. The duration was 208 degrees intake and 214 degrees exhaust. It used a .465" lift. This lobe separation puts the closing point of the exhaust valve more in the correct location to keep the air from leaving the combustion chamber while the intake port is filling it up. This keeps the incoming air in the combustion chamber when the intake valve closes to capture the high-pressure pulse from the intake port. This is why a smaller lobe separation

Figure 5.02 This is the world block being clearanced for the wider X4 industrial cam gear. Also visible is the cam retainer attached to the block.

Figure 5.03 Here is the X4 industrial double-row gear all set up.

angle of 112 to 114 degrees is fine for a carbureted intake manifold, as it has shorter runners and a faster return pulse through its runners for the same rpm. When designing a cam to optimize this pressure wave in a long runner intake, these characteristics need to be taken into consideration.

The steel roller cam used in an 8.1L has perfectly square cam lobe surfaces as compared to a flat-tappet cam that might have a 1 to 1.5-degree angle ground into the lobe. The reason for the angle in a non-roller cam is for the lobe to make a flat-tappet lifter rotate as it slides across the cam lobe. This keeps the lifter from wearing a flat spot on the lifter contact surface and keeps the cam forced to the rear of the engine. This also keeps the timing gear loaded against the thrust surface of the block and the cam from walking back and forth—which will also cause the ignition timing to vary.

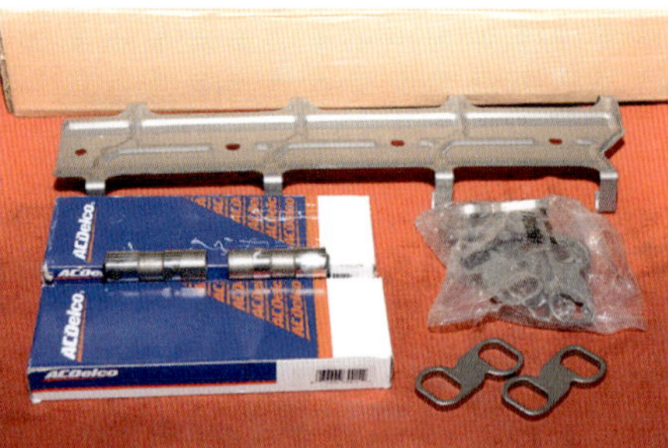

Figure 5.04 This is the GM lifter and retainer package for the big-block Chevy that uses roller lifters. It has all the parts you need. GM Part #12371056.

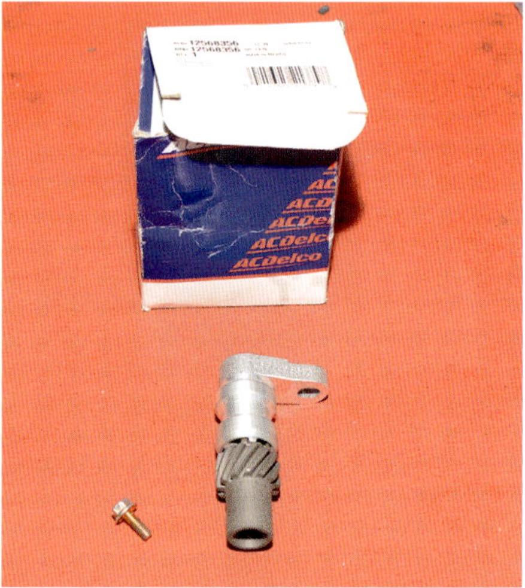

Figure 5.05 Here is the oil pump stub drive and GM box.

Because the 8.1L cam lobes are square, this doesn't load the cam forward or rearward, therefore it uses a stepped nose on the cam (Figure 5.01) and a block-mounted cam thrust plate (Figure 5.02) that is sandwiched between the cam and upper cam drive gear (Figure 5.03) to keep the cam from walking back and forth. This started in the 1996, 454 CID engine when the roller cam was introduced. The roller lifters used are the long-skirt style to keep the oil supply galley from being uncovered at full lift, therefore losing oil pressure. The lifters are held in the correct relationship to the cam by the "dog bone" lifter retainer (Figure 5.04). These retainers keep the lifter in the correct relationship to the cam lobes.

The oil pump is driven from the back of the cam by a cut-off distributor drive (Figure 5.05) that drops into the block, engages the cam oil-pump drive gear

Figure 5.06 This is a shot of the back cylinder with a stock cast piston. You can see how small the valve notch is in the piston.

which then connects to the oil-pump in the oil pan through an oil-pump drive shaft. The oil-pump shaft has a slot in one end and a tang on the other and can only be put together one way.

Camshaft Specifications

Complete books have been written on cam designs, specifications, and all aspects of the trade. Not only have there been dozens of books, there are almost an equal number of builders—Raylar, COMP Cams, Crower Cams, Schneider Cams, and the list goes on and on.

Everyone has their favorites. It is not the scope of this book to try and analyze the best cam for every application. We just hope to give you an understanding of how they are intended to work in an 8.1L engine.

In general, the stock 325 hp truck cam is 208-degree intake duration and 214-degree exhaust duration with 119-degree lobe centers and .467" lift. This is also the stock 375 hp marine cam. They are just rated differently.

The 425 hp cams went up approximately 10 degrees on both the intake and exhaust duration and the lobe centers were closed down to 114 degrees. The stock lift was .501" This worked well for a boat, but not extraordinary. You can assume that for every 10 degrees you add to the intake and exhaust duration, it will bump the cam up one level. This is a general statement as some manufacturers prefer to add more exhaust than intake. It is all up to the manufacturers and their experiences.

Figure 5.07 This is a comparison of a small valve notch to a big valve notch.

Figure 5.08 This is how the stock piston breaks. Note how close the ring groove is to the piston eyebrow. It is very thin in this area. Usually, with the cast pistons, it will also shatter the piston into tiny pieces and the rod will break the cylinder wall. This was a forged piston and didn't shatter.

The stock cast pistons have a very shallow intake valve notch in the piston and therefore limit the overall lift of the valve (Figure 5.06). For use of high valve lift and cast pistons, be sure to check the clearances between the valve and piston. If a valve hits the cast hypereutectic piston, it will shatter into a thousand pieces and let the connecting rod knock a hole in the cylinder wall. This problem is eliminated when forged aluminum pistons are installed. Think carefully before you use a cast hypereutectic piston! Forged aluminum pistons usually have a bigger intake valve notch machined into them to accommodate more lift—up to .650" (Figure 5.07, Figure 5.08).

Valve Train

Well, we have talked on and on about camshafts and so we think it's about time to turn our attention to the 8.1L valve train. From the manufacturer's

Figure 5.09 Here is the Raylar aftermarket rocker arm stud locknut. It is designed to work with stainless roller rockers. This locknut will allow the roller rockers to fit under the stock valve covers.

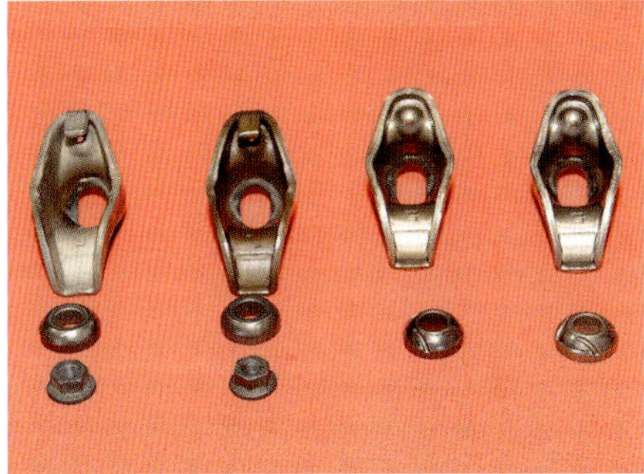

Figure 5.10 These are stock 8.1 rockers. The second from the left has turned blue from heat. The third from left had an aftermarket grooved pivot ball and also turned blue. The pivot ball and rocker arm were heated by friction to a high enough temperature that the blue color remained. This is why roller rockers are necessary in high rpm endurance engines.

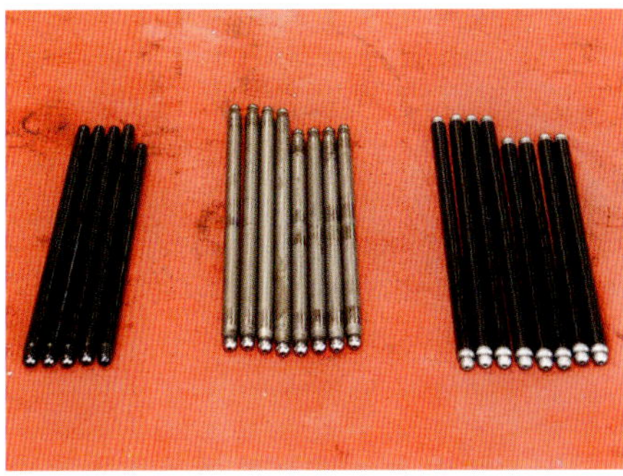

Figure 5.11 Three different makes of pushrods. The center ones are stock. The stock pushrods generally work fine except for under the harshest environments.

Figure 5.12 On the left are ARP aftermarket studs and poly locks. On the right are two stock, stamped rockers. You will notice that the right rocker in the trunnion area has turned to a blue-purple due to overheating from friction. In order to turn this color, the rocker would have turned red hot. In front are two aftermarket pivot balls with grooves for more oil.

Figure 5.13 Notice the smaller mass of the stainless-steel roller rockers in this image. The acoustic difference between the aluminum and stainless rockers is that the stainless tend to ring and the aluminum rockers have a dead sound. You can see how high the poly locknut sits above the rocker. This is what keeps the valve covers from fitting.

Figure 5.14 This is an aftermarket aluminum rocker. Their mass make them a tight fit inside the valve covers and usually requires hand-fitting.

Figure 5.15 Here is a comparison of the standard poly lock, a specialty-machined and cut-down poly lock to fit under stock 8.1 valve covers, and the Raylar locknut. The cut-down nuts require a lot of work and extra money for a minimum increase in durability.

Figure 5.16 Three roller rocker trunnions. The one on the left has the seat correct, the middle one has the trunnion upside down, and the right has the locknut for the non-adjustable stock rocker stud installed.

view, this is one of the best and most efficient systems. To become even more efficient would be to build a racing engine. Let's look at a stock 8.1L.

The valve train of the 8.1L is a non-adjustable rocker stud (Figure 5.09), stamped steel rocker with a pivot ball (Figure 5.10) and a ⅜" tubular pushrod with balls on both ends (Figure 5.11). Intake length is 8.180", exhaust length is 9.130". The rocker stud has a 10 mm metric thread that screws into the head, a 7/16" shank that registers the pivot ball and an 8mm × 1.5-metric thread retaining nut. The stamped steel rockers and pivot ball work very well in truck, low rpm industrial, and light marine applications.

Where we see the limits of durability with stamped rockers is at high rpm marine and applications with higher lift and longer duration. In this environment, the friction of the ball-to-rocker arm will turn the rockers blue from heat (Figure 5.12). If you go to higher lifts, the slots in the rockers will bind on the rocker stud and have been known to break pushrods and rockers.

The stock nonadjustable valve train is designed to simply assemble all the parts and it works quite well until you have a valve job done or install a new cam with a different lift or base circle. Then it can all go out the window. This is when people get creative and use aftermarket rocker studs, poly locks, and different pushrod lengths for different lift and base circles. When you try to compensate for these differences by moving the rocker up or down things lose their relative positions. There is a tool that can be bought from the cam suppliers that slides on the rocker stud, and rests on the tip of the valve, indicating the correct length of your needed pushrod. This gives you a very good starting point and takes a lot of the guess work out of fitting your valve train.

Roller Rockers

If you decide to install roller rockers, you can use the ARP studs for the 8.1L and fit the roller rockers in place using the adjustable poly lock nuts (Figure 5.13, Figure 5.14, Figure 5.15). This is a very durable system. The biggest issue, though, is that the poly locks stick up too high and will not let the valve covers fit on the head. This can be remedied by making/buying new, taller valve covers, having valve cover spacers made, or you can machine the studs shorter, cut down the poly locks to a shorter dimension and trial fit them until the valve covers fit. This can take a lot of time and money.

For almost all applications, the Raylar, nonadjustable, roller rockers and nuts do extremely well (Figure 5.16). You just assemble the stainless roller rockers; retainer nuts and the valve covers drop on. The Raylar rocker nuts use the stock 8.1L rocker studs and place the roller rockers in the correct location to use the stock pushrod (refer back to Figure 5.09). The valve tip height must be correct on the valves and the base circle of the cam must be the correct diameter for the dimensions to work with the stock pushrods. If the cam or valve tips are not correct, longer or shorter length pushrods can correct the problem.

If you are going all-out endurance racing, we would use the ARP studs, poly locks and a stud girdle and make it work, just for that slight edge of durability (Figure 5.17). But, again, it is a lot of time and money.

Figure 5.17 This is a custom stud girdle made by Hank Slocum for his 547 CID 8.1L engine. He used ARP rocker studs and poly locks. He was looking for the maximum durability for high rpm, .730 lift, and 270–280-degree duration cam. He also made custom spacers to raise the valve covers for clearance.

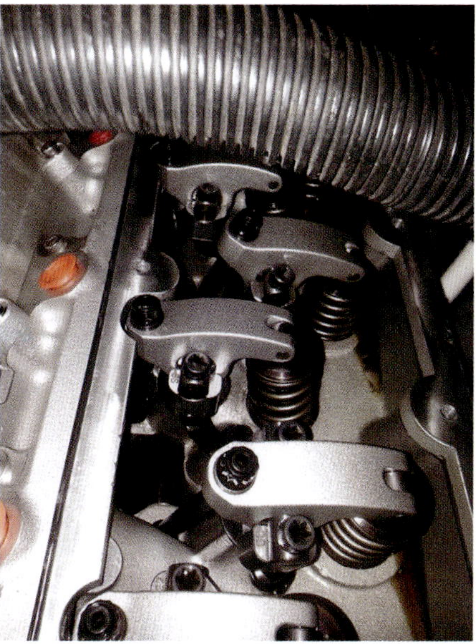

Figure 5.18 This is a Jesel shaft rocker assembly installed in Chris Lee's 547 CID 8.1L blower motor. It works extremely well; however, it was very labor intensive to install and needed custom length pushrods to fit correctly. He also needed to make spacers to raise the valve covers for clearance. Note the notches needed in the valve cover spacer rails.

6

Intakes and Fuel Injection

Theory

Larry and I are old enough to remember log-style intake manifolds with runners that simply connected the carburetor to the four, six, or eight, cylinder inline engines. There was nothing to it in those days—everything was adjusted for fit on the engine. The carburetor sat in the middle of the block and had long and short runners that simply fed gas to each cylinder. Fortunately, those days are gone and now intake runners are "tuned" for performance.

It began with the advent of fuel injection. Fuel injection provided automotive engineers the opportunity to make all of the intake runners exactly the same length, then tune them for specific rpm and torque ranges. To do this they created long runners with small cross sections, and short ones with large cross sections. Long pipes (runners) had the *small* cross section enhancing *low* rpm, and short pipes had the *larger* cross sections enhancing *high* rpm. Think back, if you can, to the 1961 Chrysler 300G. It had a carburetor over the right side of the engine that fed the *left* side valves and a carburetor over the left side feeding the *right*-side valves. The long runner length was tuned for high torque at low rpms.

The point here is that the timing of the pressure wave is generated by the *closing* of the intake valve, which then travels back the length of the runner to the runner bell. The low pressure at the bell, again, reverses the pressure wave back to the intake valve and adds to the intake runner pressure at the time of opening the intake valve. This *increases* the air density entering the cylinder. This length and cross-sectional area of the runner determines the time and rpm of the arrival of the pressure wave. Shortening the length of the runner decreases the time required and equates to a higher rpm, while lengthening the runner increases the time, thus producing a lower rpm torque.

Figure 6.01 Larry has taken the liberty of cutting an intake manifold in half, lengthwise, to show you what's happening. As you can see, the intake runner is 19" long—although it says 16" inside. (Who did this?!) The blue lines indicate where the material from the manifold will be cut out. You'll see this in the next section.

Design

Now we can discuss how the stock, 8.1L, intake manifold is made. It begins with intake runners of 19" long, inside the manifold, the 6.5" from the head of the valve to the intake surface of the head for a total of 25.5" (Figure 6.01).

Thus, the rpm of the intake is tuned for about 2800 rpm. This also happens to be where max torque is in the stock engine. To design a higher rpm intake manifold you shorten the runners. As an example, the Raylar Cool-Gap manifold has a larger runner cross section compared to the GM manifold, a length of 16", and 6.5" in the head for a total of 22.5" This now puts the rpm up to about 3500–4000 rpm. (Figure 6.02)

Raylar's prototype for the Short Runners intake manifold used an 11" runner for a total of 17.5", generating 4000–5000 rpm. (Figure 6.03) The Accel big-block Chevy Super Ram has a 9" runner for a total of 15.5" which Accel recommends for 4500–6000 rpm. You can see that there is a relationship between runner length torque and rpm. This tuned runner length

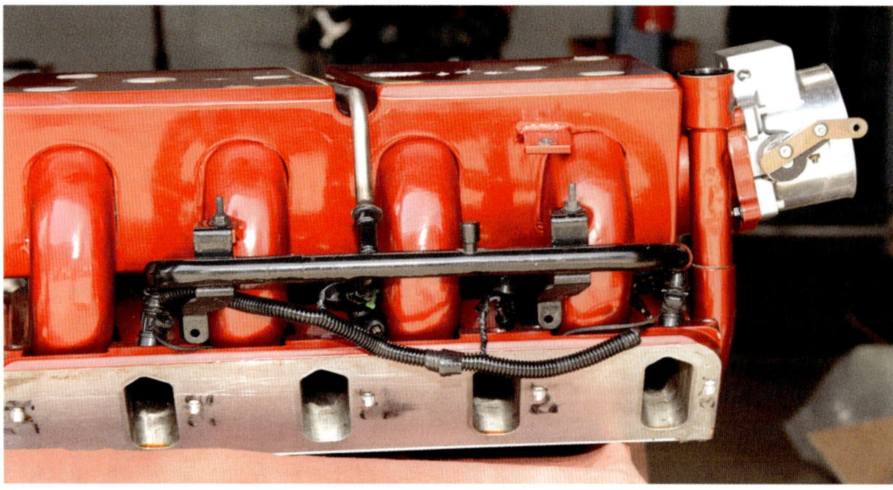

Figure 6.02 This is a side view of the Raylar Cool-Gap, 90 mm intake manifold. Although it is inside, it has a manifold runner length of 16", giving it around 3500 rpm.

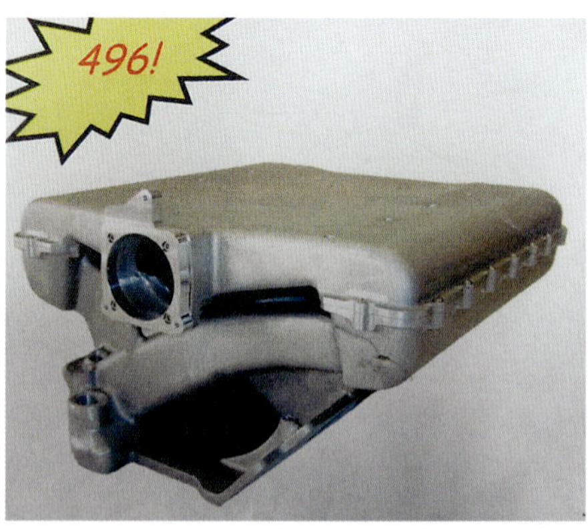

Figure 6.04 This is a photo from the Arizona Speed and Marine catalog. It shows a 90 mm flange attached. Finding one like this would be difficult as they are no longer manufactured. (Photo courtesy of Arizona Speed and Marine.)

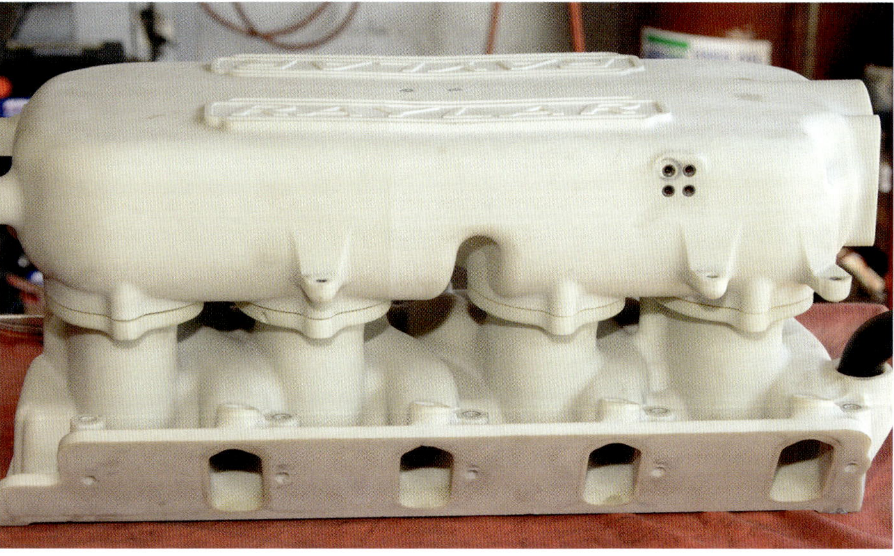

Figure 6.03 Prototype short-runner intake manifold for testing higher rpm. The reason this looks like plastic is that it is! This was printed on a 3D printer according to Larry's instructions. This manifold has many hours on the dynamometer and has performed well in the 4000–6500 rpm range.

must also work in conjunction with a cam of specific duration and lobe separation, in order to capture the intake pressure wave at the correct time for the intake valve to close, keeping the higher pressure in the cylinder.

Manifolds

In the world of 8.1L engines there are only a few choices for performance-intake manifolds. One of the first manufactured was by Arizona Speed and Marine. (Figure 6.04) It had long, big volume runners and worked much better than the stock manifolds. It was designed for offshore racing and is still in use, though it is very hard to find these days. Viewers noted that it "looked like a coffee table, sitting on top of a 496." If you can find one not being used, you have a very nice collectible.

Next is the Cool-Gap manufactured by Raylar. It is the best intake for airflow on the 496 8.1L engine within the 550–600 hp range. It was designed much like a tunnel ram but with 16", high-volume runners. The early manifold had an 80 mm throttle body and the later had a 90 mm throttle body.

The Raylar Cool-Gap intake manifold was made with only one consideration: to create the best airflow and horsepower capabilities within the parameters of a stock, 8.1L intake manifold for marine application. It wasn't designed with any considerations for compliance in a truck engine, including the need to pass emission controls or to appear as a stock part. The Cool-Gap manifold's runners are not airflow limited and the plenum area is comparable in area to the engine displacement. The limiting factor is the size of throttle body and the length of the runners for the rpm desired. There have been several variations of the Cool-Gap intakes over time, such as the twin Holley 4-bbl electronic throttle bodies mounted on top, (Figure 6.05) or the 100 mm single throttle body (Figure 6.06). For those who are building a truck and aren't limited by rules, emissions, or funds, you can still use the Cool-Gap manifold. It fits in the same space as the stock truck manifold. You will lose your EGR, EVAP, and will need to modify your wiring. The fuel rails are the same. The throttle body is at a different angle, the air intake will need some adjustments, but powder coat to match the color of your truck, and it will look extremely fine! If you find that you need to replace the fuel pressure regulator along with using the Raylar kit, and the part isn't available, then go to your favorite junk yard along with

Figure 6.05 This is the Raylar Cool-Gap manifold with twin 1000 cfm electronic, throttle bodies. This setup is still used in the marine industry.

Figure 6.07 Pictured here is the 80 mm modified stock, 8.1L. You're looking down into the ported throttle body.

Figure 6.06 This is a modified stock manifold with a 100 mm throttle body for a Camaro or Chevelle with the throttle body pointed straight forward instead of up. By positioning the throttle body straight forward, you eliminate any hood clearance issues.

a pair of snap ring pliers and a small screwdriver. Find a 1999 to 2006 small block truck—they have the same regulator and there are lots to choose from.

Next is the modified stock, 8.1L developed by Raylar (Figure 6.07). The purpose in developing this manifold was for trucks needing to retain their EVAP, PCV, EGR, and air-vacuum controls. After cutting up several stock intake manifolds, several shortcomings were apparent. These shortcomings were designed into the intake manifold for emissions. On the downside, it had limited airflow into the plenum area, and the plenum volume was too small with limited runner recovery. This in turn limited the air that was available to the intake runners (Figure 6.08). After much development, testing, and dyno time, a process was developed that allowed the intake to supply 80% as much air as the Cool-Gap manifold. This modified intake supplies the air requirements of a 450–550 hp engine. The manifold can be supplied with the 3-bolt flanges for the 80 mm throttle body, or the 4-bolt flange for the 90 mm throttle body. This manifold modification has also been adapted to the marine world with great success as a less expensive alternative to the Cool-Gap intake manifold. The modified stock manifold still leaves some horsepower on the table when compared with the Cool-Gap manifold with any cam combination.

Some of the prototype manifolds made by Raylar should also be described. First would be the individual runner, fuel injected manifold, used on the Raylar 750 hp race engine for a specific racing class in Europe during the 2008–2009 seasons (Figure 6.09). Raylar has also developed several

Figure 6.08 To allow access to the inside of the manifold, Larry cuts this bottom portion out. There is a plenum inside that he removes to allow air to move more freely. (See Sidebar on Engine Airflow for more details.)

3D-printed, short-runner intake manifolds made for dyno testing on different horsepower and rpm ranges (Figure 6.10). In addition, Raylar created several custom, cut-down stock intake manifolds, for use in Corvettes and other low-hood clearance cars (Figure 6.11).

Also, in the lineup is the Dart carbureted 8.1L intake manifolds (Figure 6.12). This manifold was developed to use a 4150- or 4160-style carburetor base. In the industrial market, it is used with propane throttle bodies. It can also be used with a simple 780

Figure 6.09 This beautiful rig shows a limited production assembly of the Raylar Stack Injection manifold used for maximum horsepower while staying naturally aspirated. It was developed for a 750 hp marine engine for use in 2008 and 2009 European class racing.

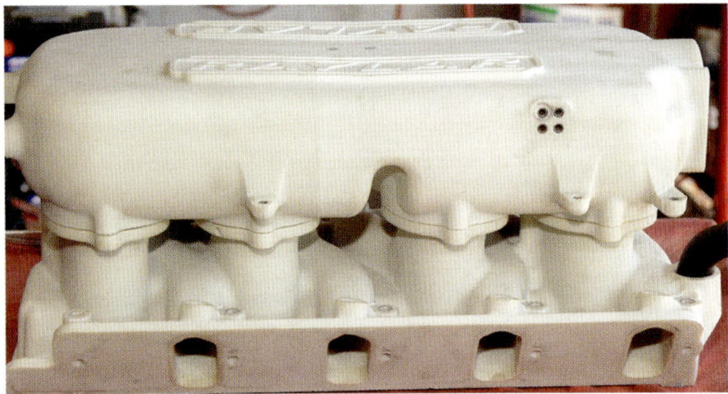

Figure 6.10 Sideview of a prototype, 11", short runner, plastic intake manifold.

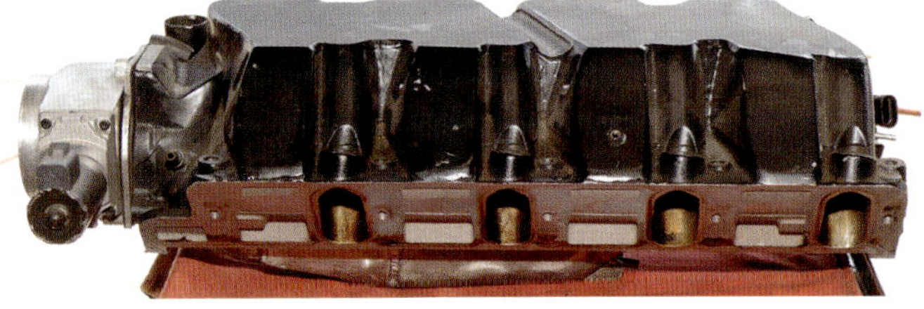

Figure 6.11 Corvettes and other low-hood clearance autos used this cut-down manifold to fit—otherwise the only other alternative was to make a hole in the hood!

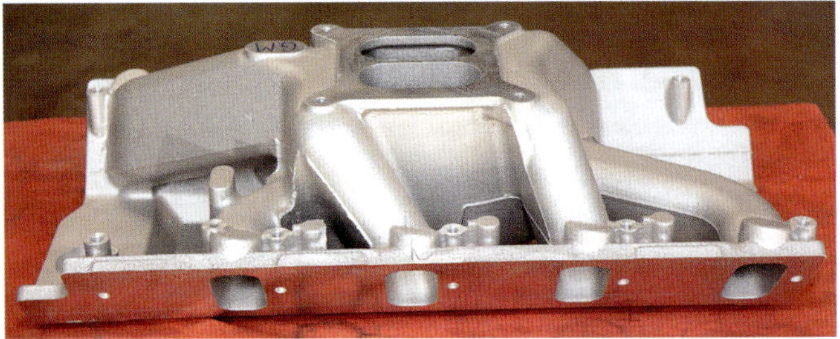

Figure 6.12 Dart carbureted 8.1L intake manifold. It can be used on GM cars with higher hood clearances. It uses a Holley 4150 base pattern.

Figure 6.13 This is a fly-by-wire throttle body used in the 2001 and 2002, 8.1L and is 78 mm.

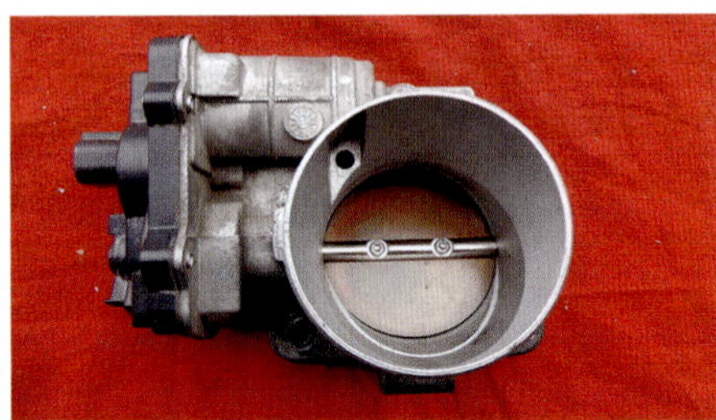

Figure 6.14 From 2003 to 2006 they used a different 78 mm fly-by-wire throttle body.

Figure 6.15 For marine use, a 78 mm throttle body with mechanical linkage was used.

cfm or 850 cfm Holley on a standard 8.1L to remove the fuel injection, or to simplify the aftermarket fuel injection units. It can be used with a GM-style distributor or an aftermarket LS1-style ignition-timing module for the X24 count reluctor by MSD, Holley, Accel, or other aftermarket ignition suppliers.

The 2001 to 2002 stock GM throttle body for the 8.1L is a 78 mm *fly-by-wire* type throttle body (Figure 6.13). The 2003 to 2006 truck also used a 78 mm fly-by-wire throttle body (Figure 6.14). The marine 496 engines used a 78 mm *cable*-actuated throttle body (Figure 6.15). The 2001 and 2002 trucks used an all-aluminum throttle body with one 6-pin wire connector going to the TPS and another 2-pin wire connector going to the throttle body

DESIGNING AN INTAKE MANIFOLD

When Raylar began to develop their own intake manifold, they created prototypes using 3D printers. First, they would design the manifold, then print the model through a 3D application and printer. The following shows the process. After the manifold was printed, they mounted it to an engine for testing, and it worked perfectly! Remember, this prototype is a plastic substrate. When everything was complete, they had it cast in aluminum.

Figure S6.01 Though you have seen this photo in the chapter text, this is what the completed part looked like after 3D printing. It is a two-part assembly and both the top and bottom parts are shown here.

Figure S6.02 This is the bottom half of the manifold. The black rings around each of the intakes were not printed; they were installed after the printing was completed.

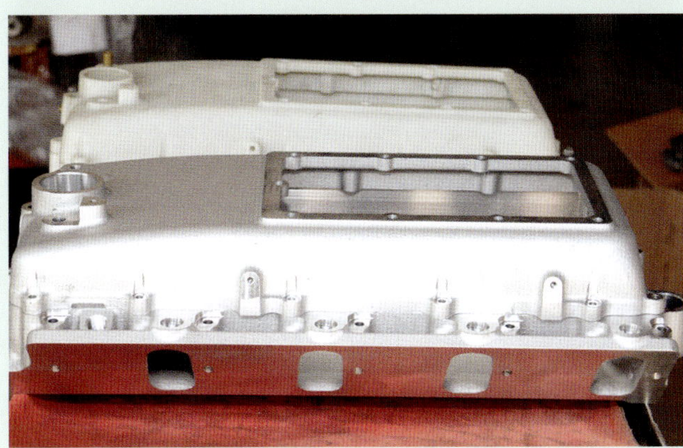

Figure S6.03 and Figure S6.04 The plastic 3D printed model of this supercharger manifold was used as the original for a mold, and then cast in aluminum.

motor. From 2003 until 2008 it used a half black plastic and half aluminum throttle body with a single 8-pin wire connector.

Next, we have the BBK Performance Parts 80 mm throttle body for fly-by-wire (1756 or 1757). From there we go to the 90 mm. It's interesting to note that all GM 5.3L, 6L, and 6.2L trucks after 2006 use a 90 mm throttle body, while the 8.1L is much larger in displacement and uses a 78 mm throttle body. It seems that if the LS engine needed a 90 mm throttle body, the 8.1L definitely could use the 90 mm! For the early 2001 and 2002 trucks, the Corvette 90 mm throttle body is the one of choice (Figure 6.16). For 2003 to 2006 trucks, the 90 mm truck throttle body should be used (Figure 6.17). If you're going for the marine application, specifically the marine 80 mm, 3-bolt and the 90 mm 4-bolt cable operated throttle bodies, Raylar has custom billet throttle bodies available (Figure 6.18). We have seen people modify the Camaro cable throttle body as well.

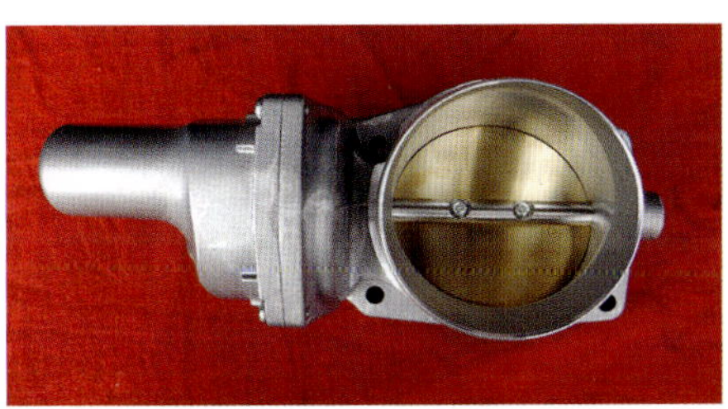

Figure 6.16 In 2001 and 2002 a 90 mm Corvette throttle body was the best choice.

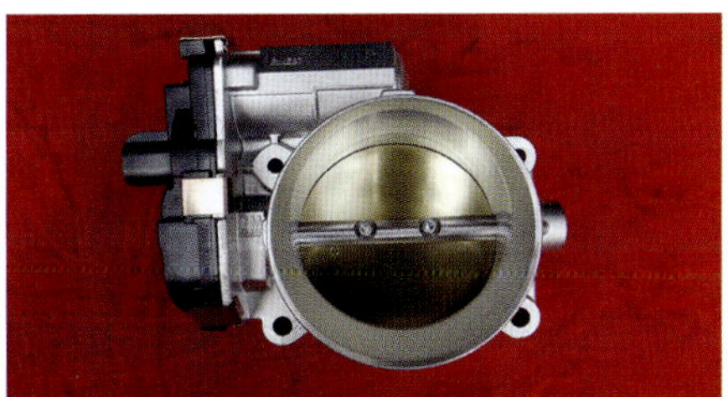

Figure 6.17 For the 2003 to 2006 8.1L upgrade, the 90 mm truck throttle body is the best choice.

ENGINE AIRFLOW

One of the most important features of the "big" engine is airflow. Every advantage must be considered while the engine is in development. This, however, must be balanced with awareness of the emissions that increased airflow pushes into the atmosphere. Some states have strict emissions control on both cars and trucks while other states often ignore trucks. If you have any doubts about emission controls in your state or county, contact the appropriate agency and learn the correct legal requirements for your area. Why are we mentioning this? What we're about to show you will increase your emissions by about five points. With many of the other tricks we've shown you, your emissions could be off the charts. "Foretold is forewarned."

When working on a stock intake manifold there are internal cast plenums installed by the factory engineers that decrease airflow. Designed into the intake manifold is an EGR (Exhaust Gas Recirculation) port used for re-introducing exhaust gasses back into the intake manifold. For this port to work well, they designed a venturi (or plenum) inside the intake manifold to draw the EGR gasses in. This venturi causes the restriction. The exhaust gasses lean out the fuel/air ratio even further for emissions reasons.

To remove the wall to access the EGR port, use a metal cutting saber saw, cutting out the lower front section (bottom) in the pattern shown (Figure S6.05). Note that the piece cut from the body of the intake manifold is lying on top of the cutout portion. Insert a longer metal cutting blade in your saw and remove the interior wall just below the area you've cut. Now your manifold should look like this: (Figure S6.06). With a file or die grinder, smooth out the rough edges. The crystalline marks in the upper right corner are from the die grinder used to smooth the rough edges. Remember, we're trying to move as much air as quickly as possible. Rough edges will slow air down.

Now that we've finished cutting things up, the first plate you removed must be welded back into place. Larry gave the project to one of the "free world's greatest welders," Bob "the god" Lee (Figure S6.07). Thanks Bob, you did a splendid job!

Figure S6.05 This shows the piece of material that needs to be removed from the bottom of the GM manifold to access the inner restriction. It will be re-welded back in place.

Figure S6.06 This photo shows the inner restriction removed.

Figure S6.07 This is Bob "the god" Lee, the best welder ever, putting the parts and pieces back together.

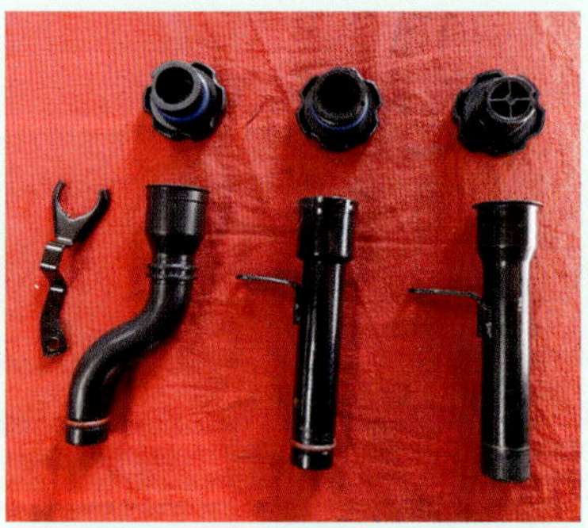

Figure S6.08 This photo illustrates the three different oil fillers for the 8.1L. First tube on the left is the 2004 and up truck plastic oil filler. The middle tube is a 2004 and up marine oil filler. Note that both 2004 and up tubes have O-rings to seal them. The last tube on the right is the 2001 to 2004 marine and truck oil fill tube. Note that this tube is glued into the manifold.

Figure 6.18 For custom marine manifolds, Raylar makes 80 mm and 90 mm polished billet throttle bodies. This is an 80 mm throttle body.

Figure 6.19 Here is a shot of Quinton Eilert's 577 CID supercharger installed in his 2500 series truck.

Figure 6.20 A side view of a Whipple marine supercharger installed by Raylar. The early kit provided a 2.3L blower while the later kit provided 3.3L.

Figure 6.21 Although it looks quite similar to the previous marine supercharger, this is a low-profile 8.1L truck unit. It uses the 2.9L supercharger and is required for clearance under the 2001 and up truck firewall.

The unlimited Raylar Cool-Gap manifold uses two Holley-type 1000 cfm electronic throttle bodies mounted on top of the plenum. It still uses the factory fuel injection rails and electrical system. This allows the same computer plug-in for marine or truck applications. (Refer back to Figure 6.05)

Superchargers

History

From 2001 to 2004 Whipple Superchargers made a 2.3L supercharger kit for the 8.1L truck engine. It mounted a small supercharger where the alternator originally sat. From there, the air was moved through an intercooler sitting above and behind the engine. The air flowed back around to the front and into the stock intake manifold. This was normal for the level of development at that time. It had several airflow limitations in size and flow, but it's what they had. If you are supercharging, any improvement in airflow is a good thing. This early supercharger overcame several limitations in the 8.1L intake manifold and heads. In recent years there have been substantial improvements in design and installation techniques. These have removed the restrictions in the air intake, heat exchangers, and increased the displacement of the superchargers (2.9L). All of these improvements have greatly improved torque and horsepower outputs and have allowed the stock fuel injection computer to be utilized, making it much easier to program (Figure 6.19).

Marine

Currently there are two marine supercharger kits available. The first marine kit produced by Whipple Superchargers used a 2.3L blower and the later kit uses a 3.3L blower (Figure 6.20). This has a rear-mounted air intake with eight injectors spraying fuel directly into the supercharger air intake. This works extremely well in the marine and airboat world. It does not work so well in the 2001 to current truck world. The rear-mounted air intake runs directly into the firewall. You can guess what that does.

STACK INJECTIONS

Sometimes in the development of an engine, you may need it naturally aspirated, yet want to gain maximum power and outrageous looks. Yes, superchargers will make more power, but when this is not an option, individual runner (stack injection) manifold designs are the only choice. These designs depend on Mother Nature's natural air pressure to fill the voids caused by the piston moving down the cylinder and creating a vacuum or low-pressure area. To get the most power this way, you want the air to reach the cylinders with the least amount of restriction.

In the '40s '50s and '60s, the standard production intake manifold was just a way to connect the carburetor to the cylinder, without a lot of regard to the engineering or design of the manifold. It could have one, two, or even three 90-degree bends in the air flow before

Figure-S6-09 Here is the manifold and bed plate in the mill at Mark Johnson's machine shop in Colorado being measured for the bolt hole configurations. Mark has already machined the velocity stacks that go on top of the throttle bodies. The first grouping of countersunk holes is from the bed plate into the top of the runner flanges under the bedplate. This is to keep the gaskets on the bottom side of the bedplate from moving. This grouping of four bolts is indexed at 15 degrees off axis to allow the throttle body bolts to be attached to the bedplate on axis. At this point the runners and flanges are completely welded together. This is done on a jig at Bob Lee's to keep the flanges and runners square with each other. (Photo courtesy of Mark Johnson.)

Figure-S6-10 In this photo the pair of throttle bodies are being indexed to match the port runner location. It happens to be on the same centerline as the engine block bore centers, 4.840". Here, the couplers between the individual throttle bodies are being fit. Also, you can see the idle bypass ports that allow each throttle body to be adjusted separately from one another. This makes individual port airflow a snap.

Truck

Enter supercharger kit number two (Figure 6.21). This kit is produced by Raylar and uses the 2.9L supercharger body. The 3.3L was the first choice but would not fit under the truck firewall, and in the same space as the stock intake manifold. This placement was a requirement for it to be a plug-and-play supercharger kit. It uses a newly designed intake manifold base that puts the supercharger between the heads and includes an intercooler core inside the manifold for low installed heights and ease of installation. It is similar in design to the Whipple LS supercharger truck kit.

Other Superchargers

There have also been other supercharger kits available, such as Vortex, Procharger, and STS turbo. Some of these kits might become available on the internet from time to time, but these kits are no longer available new.

Also keep in mind that a positive displacement supercharger or a belt-driven centrifugal supercharger that is driven to produce enough air to make 600 crankshaft horsepower, generally requires an additional 60 to 100 hp of load to drive the supercharger. This means that your stock cast 496 pistons, rods, and crank would be loaded at 650–700 hp.

STACK INJECTIONS (continued)

the air/fuel mixture reached the cylinders. For reference, for every 90-degree turn there is a 10% loss in air flow.

The first person to recognize the performance potential of an individual runner intake manifold was Stu Hilborn. He designed a manifold with straight runners for the Ford V8 flathead engine in the late '40s. It was first used at the Bonneville races, and was very crude by today's standards. It was simply eight tubes with throttle plates in each individual runner going into each cylinder. Fuel was pumped into each runner just below the throttle plate. But it made much more power! Soon it was standard equipment on just about every Offenhauser race engine. In the '50s Hilborn was the go-to source for race type individual runner intake manifolds. During the '60s and '70s the design was improved and reengineered by many different manufacturers such as Kinsler, Crower, Inglese, and Enderle, to be the style of intake that would produce the most power at wide open throttle on any naturally aspirated engine. In the early days of fuel injection, with the barrel valve controlling fuel delivery, the drivability left a lot to be desired. Yes, with the Lucas fuel metering system, the drivability could be worked out, but at a very high cost.

With the advent of CNC machining and electronic fuel controls, the coolest intakes imaginable can be made. The CNC machining can make very intricate pieces that create manifolds and throttle bodies for just about any imaginable combination. The old players like Kinsler, Hilborn, and Crower are still here, but there are a lot of new players. Borla, Speedmaster, F&B (where I got mine), EFI, and Fox to name a few. These companies are machining manifolds and parts for just about any engine. With the multitude of aftermarket Electronic Fuel Injection control systems to work with, in conjunction with manifolds, it is easy to manage fuel and air. With this technology, it is easy to create an exotic looking intake generating maximum power, but which is still civilized for everyday driving.

There are three sets of the stack injection featured on the front cover. The original was made for a class of racing in Europe. It required a stock-style fuel injected engine, non-supercharged, "run what you brung," engine. A 496-style engine was built using a GM 572 short block, large port CNC Raylar aluminum heads with 2.300 intake and 1.800 exhaust valves. The manifold was built using the Cool-Gap CNC manifold flanges, specially cast intake runners, and custom individual throttle bodies. The ¾" base plate has a large area machined out under the bottom to make a vacuum chamber for the IAC and MAP sensors to operate. Again, it was assembled and welded by Bob Lee. This engine made 750 hp and is as close to a big block Chevy Can-Am intake for a 496 as there ever will be. Way Kool!

The images included here showcase some of Larry's extraordinary experiences regarding these units.

Figure-S6-11 The throttle bodies are all located on the plate and the outside perimeter shape is being decided. This shape needs to include considerations for fuel rail clearances, linkage, and computer sensors. Lying in front of the manifold is the cover for the vacuum reservoir that is machined into the bottom of the bed plate for port balancing and the MAP sensor.

Figure-S6-12 This is a 750 hp race engine in Harnestad, Sweden. The stack injection system is being worked on and "refreshed." It sits on a dynamometer in Martin Lundkvist's shop. He tells us it still runs strong. (Photo courtesy of Martin Lundkvist.)

7

Computers

A Brief History

It's always fun to take a quick look into the past to see how things were built before we were born or when we were very young—the automobile computer is one of those things. Larry and I looked up the early use of fuel injection for automobiles and found the following information.

The first attempt at computerized fuel injection on an American car was in 1957. The Bendix Motor Corp. had been working on an injection system they called the "Electrojector" and the American Motor Company decided to try it on their 5.4L V8 Rambler Rebel. This initial attempt for the first electronic fuel injection (EFI) system was a disaster. Components of the computer were so sensitive that cold weather would cause it to fail. Remember, this was an analog system composed of vacuum tubes and paper-wound condensers. Finally, during pre-production testing the engineers had to throw up their hands and return to carburetion.

Bendix continued to work on this project and found another buyer. In 1958 Chrysler picked it up for the Chrysler 300D, the DeSoto Adventurer, the Dodge D500, and the Plymouth Fury. Again, due to the primitive nature of this project, only 35 of these cars were delivered, and after many problems, were eventually retrofitted with carburetors. Bendix finally sold the patent rights to Bosch.

By 1967 the Electrojector, developed by Bosch, had evolved into a marketable project and was renamed as the D-Jectronic. This EFI system was introduced on the Volkswagen in 1968 and followed up by the K-Jectronic and L-Jectronic into the mid-1970s. By then, Citroen, Saab, Mercedes-Benz, Volvo, and Jaguar had adopted this new technology. Soon, the Japanese jumped on the EFI bandwagon and the rest is pretty much history.

Computers and Binary Code

Computers use *binary code* to store data. Binary numbers are simply zeros (0) and ones (1) and strung into combinations. The computer sees the (0) as off and the (1) as on, or "yes" and "no" through its processor. Here is the binary number pattern of zero through 10.

Decimal pattern	Binary pattern
0	0
1	1
2	10
3	11
4	100
5	101
6	110
7	111
8	1000
9	1001
10	1010

To understand the binary system a little better, let's try learning to count in that system. But first let's try counting in the decimal system. Decimal counting uses the old-fashioned "ten-finger" example: 0–9. Counting begins by dropping the last two numbers to the right when it reaches "nine." 000, 001, 002, 003–009. Then, drop the "9" and "0" and add "10"—010, 011, 012, etc. When you reach the last of the "nines" you drop the right two numbers and increase the leftmost—097, 098, 099, 100, 101, 102.

Binary counting follows the same procedures, except only two symbols are available, 0 and 1. After a digit in binary reaches "1" in its next iteration it is reset to "0" but also causes an increment of the next digit to the left:

0000

0001 (rightmost digit starts over, and the next digit is incremented)

0010, 0011 (right two digits start over and next digit is incremented)

0100, 0101, 0110, 0111 (right three digits start over and the next is incremented)

1000, 1001, 1010, 1011, 1101, 1110, 1111…

How the Computer Works

Let's begin by looking at the illustration of an X58 count crankshaft reluctor (Figure 7.01). This reluctor has 57 teeth and 58 valleys and then a solid area the width of three teeth and valleys for restart references. The pick-up is the long black sensor that inserts in the rear of the block (Figure 7.02). As the crankshaft starts to turn the reluctor, the computer locates Top Dead Center (TDC) based on the three solid teeth. As the crankshaft continues its rotation, the pick-up reads the first valley as "1" and reads the first tooth as "0". The crank is designed with the first tooth sitting at TDC. Because this is a four-cycle engine (intake, compression, power, and exhaust) the reluctor must rotate two times to offer the computer all the information for one complete power stroke. The pick-up "reads" this information at 6-degree increments of rotation and sends this information to

Figure 7.01 Here's a full view of a X58 count, 8.1L reluctor. It requires its own specific crankshaft sensor that fits the 8.1L block and reads the reluctor correctly. It too, is fragile when being removed.

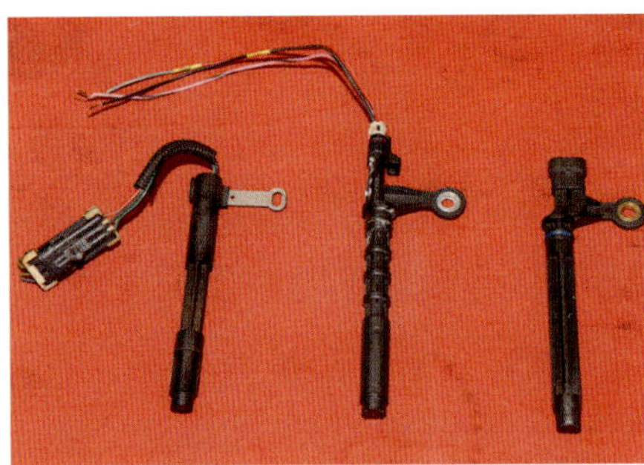

Figure 7.02 Now we have the crankshaft sensors. The first on the left is a hand-made prototype used in a 1996 8.1L block—it worked very well. In the middle is an early factory-made sensor and to the right is the current replacement General Motors sensor.

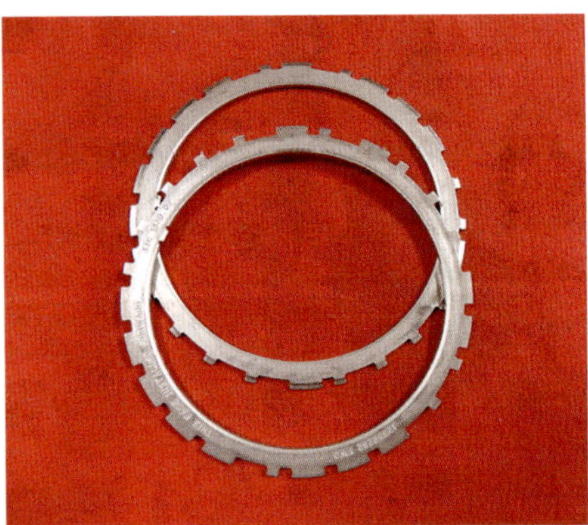

Figure 7.03 We show here the X24 count, General Motors crankshaft-timing reluctors. These are very, very fragile when being removed! For your convenience, they are listed as FWD and AFT.

the computer. Two rotations, (X58)—tooth, valley, tooth, valley, etc.

In the days before computers, the engine would simply stop when the ignition was turned off and then the mechanic would have to "hunt" for TDC. Now, the computer just finds it automatically.

The standard X24 count crankshaft reluctors (Figure 7.03) have a more complicated signal output as it supplies two different signals to the computer: one every 15 degrees of rotation and another that is an irregular pulse output used for emission references. With the above background information, we can now look at the various computers—automotive, truck, marine, and custom applications.

Computers and Fuel Injection

Throughout this chapter we're not going to try to tell you how to program a computer, rather we're simply going to talk about them and their components as they relate to the engine.

With the introduction of the Gen 7, big-block series in 2001, General Motors adopted a new configuration. Unlike the Gen 4, 5, and 6, the Gen 7 employed a computer system for fuel injection and engine control. The Gen 7 was never offered with carburetion.

The three most common computers used were the GM Delco 0411 and 4896, the MEFI 4 (Multi-Electronic-Fuel-Injection), and the Motorola 555. All of these systems are programmable for changes to the engine. The most difficult to tune is the Motorola as Mercury decided to keep the tuning program proprietary.

Automotive Computers

The Gen 7, 8.1L engine was developed in the same time frame as the GM LS1 small-block engine. This was a desirable circumstance as the technologies were the same. The programming for a 496 CID 8.1L is just the same as for a Corvette or a Camaro computer. Life is getting pretty sweet . . . If you are building a supercharged 8.1L, you would tune it with Hewlett Packard (HP) tuners or EFI Live tuning programs just as you would with a supercharged Corvette or Camaro.

There are a couple of differences between the 8.1L truck computer and that used on an automotive LS1. The truck computer has torque management installed to limit the 8.1L engine's torque from breaking the drive train. The truck's computer also has many more layers of knock control. Other than these differences, they are very much the same.

Almost all GM computers can be configured to operate an 8.1L engine. We checked on the internet for aftermarket LS1 and LS3 computers that can be configured to run the 8.1L and found a number of them available for under $1,000. This may seem a bit steep, but remember, when they were invented back in the '70s and '80s, buying them on the aftermarket would have set you back thousands of dollars.

When buying an aftermarket product, you must be sure that you have the correct crank trigger input. The X24 count crank is standard for the 8.1L and works with any of the 1997 to 2004 GM computers. For the X58 count signals, the GM E38 or E67 computer make the best sense. The X58 count crankshaft components from Raylar are from an aftermarket engine manufacturer that produces the crank reluctor and matching crank sensor for its own engines. The X58 count reluctor and sensor is completely compatible with the standard 8.1L crankshaft and can be used in any Gen 7 designed engine. To operate a later computer and six speed automatic transmission, you need an X58 count crankshaft output and X4 camshaft sensor output.

General Motors (PN 19260247) and EFI Connection both offer a front crank mounted, X58 count timing cover kit and sensor package for the Gen 5 and Gen 6 big-blocks, however, the front timing-cover-to-oil-pan radius will not fit the 8.1L oil pan without some custom work being done.

Marine Computers

Mercury Marine began using the Motorola 555 computer with the standard X24 count timing reluctor and the 1X camshaft signal, both with the 496 CID Mag and High Output engines and the Mercury Marine 525 hp Blue engine. This computer setup worked well in almost all applications. Whipple Supercharger Co. was the first to be licensed by Mercury Marine for custom tuning the Motorola computer. Prior to this time, all the programming on the Motorola computer was through Mercury.

Volvo, Marine Power, and some of the Pleasurecraft, all used the MEFI four, five, and six computers. These were also used by General Motors on the 350 CID and 502 CID Ram Jet crate engines. Various companies have been able to program this computer for years, such as Arizona Speed and Marine, Boostpower, and MEFI Burn. If you need to reprogram this computer, you can find someone online to do it for you. If you're really sharp with computers, you can also buy the programming system directly online. What a joy the Internet has become! From 2001 through 2008, Mercury Marine used a front timing cover and front crankshaft mounted X24 count crank reluctor on its 525 hp Blue engines. This package also worked using the Motorola 555 computer.

Thus far, we've talked about the invention of the computer, binary codes, how the computer actually works, and a few of its current applications. Now let's turn our attention to the fun stuff—how we can use a computer in a custom project.

Custom Computer Projects

Larry and I consider a custom computer project to be one in which you have the engine and no supporting computer. These are projects like hot rods, Chevelles, Camaros, airboats, etc. For these projects it might be easier to start with an aftermarket computer (usually cheaper) and a prepared wiring loom. With the popularity of the LS1 to LS3, most of the aftermarket computers are quite good—Holley, FAST, Accel, Edelbrock, and MSD to name a few. Many of these companies will build a wiring loom for your standard market vehicle if they don't already stock it (Figure 7.04)

Larry and I spend most of the day on the computer searching for information—that's why we often suggest certain sites. Larry found one a couple of months ago that he says is an excellent source, LS1swap.com. We also recommend David Vizard's book *Chevy Big-Blocks.* It's truly comprehensive.

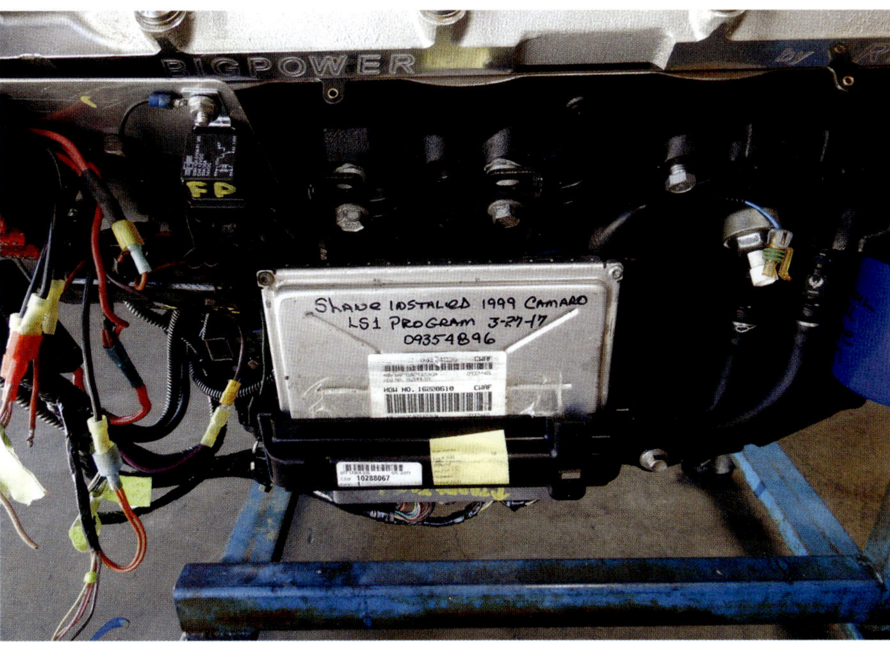

Figure 7.04 This is where the computer ended up. Larry and Shane mounted it in a 496 CID marine fuel pump bracket—it worked out very well.

The 8.1L Crankshaft Reluctors and Components

The 8.1L comes with the normal X24 count (Refer back to Figure 7.03) crankshaft timing reluctors and the 1X (Figure 7.05) camshaft gear. The 360 degrees of the rotation of the crankshaft is broken up into 15-degree segments (360 ÷ 15 = 24 => X24). These 15-degree segments tell the computer where Top Dead Center is for every rotation of the crank to initiate the timing process. (When you look at the irregular spacing of the teeth on the reluctors you wonder "How does it manage to do that?", but the computer sees what it needs to see).

As stated at the beginning of this chapter, there are four cycles required to complete the power stroke for each cylinder. The crank requires two complete revolutions to accomplish this cycle. Because the crank must rotate 720 degrees to perform these four cycles, the computer must "know" which of the two revolutions (720 ÷ 2 = 360) of the crank will be at compression, TDC, and ignition. The computer works in conjunction with the crankshaft sensor and camshaft sensor to determine this location, as the camshaft turns at half the engine speed.

Figure 7.05 In 2004 the engineers changed their mind again and decided to stamp and machine the gear to work as an "on/off" switch.

The X24 count (Refer back to Figure 7.03) and the X58 count (Refer back to Figure 7.01) crankshaft reluctor rings for the 8.1L are made of sintered metal. The X24 count has two rings labeled *fore* and *aft*. Obviously, the fore ring goes to the front and the aft ring to the rear. The X58 is labeled *crank side.* These rings are formed with notches on the outside diameter in the correct sequence for the computer to read.

These rings are also indexed to the crankshaft by a machined groove in the crankshaft that lines up with TDC, number one rod journal. There is a corresponding tang on the inner diameter of the reluctors that fits into this machined groove to exactly align with TDC, number one cylinder.

These reluctor rings press onto the rear of the crankshaft with a .002 interference fit. *These rings are fragile and should be removed and replaced gently*! If you've worked on both the LS series and the 8.1L, then you realize the reluctors on the LS are welded to the crank. However, both types of reluctors offer the same crankshaft information to the computer. During the evolution of the 8.1L, there have been several crankshaft sensor part numbers, although they are completely interchangeable throughout. Even the wiring connections at the connector remained the same (Refer back to Figure 7.02). These part numbers are: GM 12556427, GM 12576123, and GM 12575172.

The 8.1L Cam Reluctors and Components

The camshaft sensor combinations from General Motors are another matter. I'm still in wonder at the different configurations made during the early life of the 8.1L. There must have been some engineering improvements early on, but they're sure not obvious.

The very first camshaft sensor location used in the 8.1L came from the back of the block, just under the rear China rail and below the intake manifold. (Figure 7.06 and Figure 7.07) The reluctor was a half-moon shaped disc—.250" thick, attached to the top of the oil pump drive assembly and rotated at half engine speed, giving the computer the correct TDC information. This produced a positive and negative, on/off, square wave output. This configuration was similar to the early LS1. For the next three versions the sensor was moved to the front of the engine in the timing chain cover. Fortunately, this worked well and there the sensor remains. (Figure 7.08).

The cam gears and sensors are another story. For the gears, there are two completely parallel lines. The single row chain is used in the trucks and the double row chain is used in the industrial and marine engines (Figure 7.09). These X1 gears and cam sensors (Figure 7.10) are used in conjunction with the X24 count crankshaft reluctors. There are specific gears for 2001 (Figure 7.11), 2002–2003 (Figure 7.12), and 2004–2009 (Refer back to Figure 7.05). Also, introduced in 2014 for use with the X58 count crankshaft timing reluctors, there is a double row timing chain and X4 cam gear (Figure 7.13) that can be used with the later computers that reads the X58 sensor input.

Figure 7.06 This is an example of the 1996–2000 8.1L prototype motors and their camshaft sensor location in the rear China rail.

Figure 7.07 This is the inside view of the rear camshaft sensor for the prototype engine.

Figure 7.08 To the lower right is the 2004 and up camshaft sensor installed on the front timing chain cover. This is installed in a prototype 8.1L World block.

Figure 7.09 Here we have the two types of chains: single row and double row. The single row is used in the truck and commercial vehicles while the double row chain serves the marine/industrial market. When working with the double row chain, be sure to check the clearance between the chain and block to ensure there's no binding.

Figure 7.10 "The magic camshaft sensors." From left to right: the white sensor is the 2001 and is very hard to find; the black sensor is the 2002–2003 and is quickly becoming obsolete; the tall beige sensor began in 2004 and is available still through General Motors and your local auto parts store.

Figure 7.11 We've laid out a 2001 truck gear to explain a couple of things: first, this gear is one of the earliest gear/reluctor combinations. Note that when it was stamped, half of the outer edge was made thinner than its corresponding other half. A magnetic sensor distinguishes the thicker part from the thinner part and thus creates the on/off cycle. Note also the center hole. To your right it's carved out to receive the dowel on the camshaft. Be sure these two are aligned.

Figure 7.12 This gear is two years newer than the 2001 gear. However, carefully note the machined groove in the thick half of the gear. This style made the sensor "flip/flop" as compared to the 2001 gear that was designed as simply "on/off."

Figure 7.14 We've now graduated to the 2004 and later marine double-row gear. It is machined with a deeper groove, but it still serves the on/off-type sensor.

Figure 7.13 The chain and gear set on the left is the standard 2004 and later industrial camshaft and crankshaft gear with three keyways for degreeing the camshaft. The chain and gear on the right is the General Motors X4 big-block camshaft gear (PN 19256787) for use with the X58 count crankshaft timing reluctor. On the X4 camshaft gear you will see four spaces machined into the gear. These are manufactured to act as the camshaft reluctor—on/off.

The camshaft sensors also came in three versions:

Camshaft Sensors

Years	*Part Description*	*Part Number*
2001	Black GM	12572656 12575182
2002–2003	Mercury	881666 (Quicksilver)
2002–2003	White GM	12572657 12575183
2004–2010	Tall Black GM	12568983
	Tall Beige GM	12585545
	Tall Beige GM	12591720

Front Covers

Part Description	*GM Part Number*	*Mercury Part Number*
Short Cam Sensor 2001–2003	12566115	881656
Tall Cam Sensor 2004–2010	12589848	892616001

These sensors are not interchangeable because of their digital outputs—so this is where the fun begins. The three single row timing chain gears, 2001–2009 all look the same and will interchange perfectly, but will not produce the same sensor reading to the camshaft sensors due to the difference in the location and machining of the groove in the perimeter of the gear (Figure 7.14). This is the same for the 2001–2003 camshaft sensors. The sensors look exactly alike and will fit correctly from one year to the next. However, they do not produce the correct digital output when used with the incorrect camshaft gear. The same thing happens when a 2004–2009 timing cover and sensor are used to replace a damaged or missing cover on a 2001–2003. It is important to keep the timing cover, sensor, and gear that come with your engine together as a package.

If you want to update the camshaft sensor, you need to purchase the 2004 and up sensor, timing cover and the upper camshaft gear as a complete package. If you want to change the chain, use a double or single row timing chain from a 454 CID or from a 502 CID as a replacement. Actually, the upper and lower gears should last forever unless you're in a wreck, and then… We've seen broken teeth on the double row camshaft gears but not on the single row gears. There are aftermarket chain sets made for the 8.1L by S.A. Gears, CNS Motors, Cloyes, and others—but you must make sure of the application. Even then, there's no guarantee that the sensor will read the reluctor correctly. If it doesn't read the reluctor correctly, you get to pull the front of the engine back off and replace the cam gear. Doesn't this make a good case for using the original gears unless they're broken or worn beyond use?

Timing Gears

The timing chain and gears used in the Gen 7 engines are a carryover from the Gen 4, 5, and 6 engines. The distance between the crankshaft and camshaft centerlines has remained the same, so the crankshaft gear and chain can be used from the earlier short blocks. Remember, there are several dimensions in the back spacing of the crankshaft drive gear. It's best to stay with the 8.1L-specific parts.

The camshaft drive gears are another matter. The camshaft drive gear is used with the camshaft-timing sensor to produce an X1 camshaft signal. The front of the camshaft gear is machined to work with a specific sensor to generate a square wave signal that's used by the computer to determine TDC on number one cylinder, to fire the spark plug. The camshaft gear helps the cam sensor generate this signal through the magnetic conductivity of the gear.

Essentially, if the gear in front of the sensor was always a solid disc of metal, there would be no variation in magnetism—therefore, no change in the signal going to the computer. To overcome this, the engineers took a solid disc and machined away 180 degrees of the disc where the sensor reads. Now, as the camshaft gear turns, half of the disc will generate magnetism to the sensor and the other half won't. This in turn makes the sensor turn on and off, generating a square wave signal to the computer. This is how the prototype 1996–2001 engine camshaft sensors worked.

In 2002–2003 the engineers needed to make a change—probably for a good reason but neither of us know why. Instead of magnetism just being there or not being there, they machined a mirror image of a groove on the opposite side of the gear. Now, in addition to being an on/off switch, it "flip/flopped" the magnetic signal. For all the extra work, it was still just a square wave signal to the computer.

In 2004, the engineers changed their minds again and went back to the era of full magnetism, on/off. It remained this way until 2009. This makes a total of six different cam gears used from 2001–2009. To keep everyone confused, in 2014 GM added a X4 camshaft gear that uses a double row chain for the X58 count crankshaft timing reluctor and the E38 or E67 computers.

X58 Count Front Covers

This section is for the individual who wants to use the front mounted X58 reluctor. This reluctor is spaced between the damper and lower timing chain gear. Therefore, the damper needs to be shortened the thickness of the reluctor for the belts to properly align. Likewise, the front oil pan seal radius on the timing cover needs to be modified. The Gen 5 and 6 timing cover has a groove for a lip seal to mate to the oil pan—but this doesn't work with the 8.1L oil pan. The radius is the same as the 8.1L but the 8.1L pan needs a smooth surface to seal its O-ring pan gasket. Larry corrected this problem years ago by cutting a section of aluminum from a ⅜" plate in a moon shape that fit the groove of the timing cover. This in turn was JB-welded into the groove in the cover and finished to a smooth surface for the 8.1L gasket to seat on. Mercury Marine has used this same timing cover arrangement on its Gen 6, 525 hp Blue engine with a X24 count reluctor since 2002.

After you have installed the X58 count crankshaft pickup, the next item is the X4 camshaft gear from GM. (Refer back to Figure 7.12) It has been used on their 8.0L industrial engines since 2014. It works well in conjunction with the 2004 and up 8.1L timing cover and camshaft sensor. If you're using this, pay particular attention to back clearances with the chain installed. Larry has had interference issues and needed to modify the front bulkhead of the block for clearances. Check Chapter 2, Big-Block Indentification. There's a picture of the front of the block and camshaft retainer. Metal must be removed where you see the yellow paint (Figure 7.15).

Figure 7.15 These are the yellow marks Larry made where metal had to be ground away to allow for clearance of the double row chain.

Figure 7.16 Obviously, a PSI short block with the 4.350" bore. There are a couple of interesting features though. It has the 2004 and later front timing cover and sensor and the broached groove in the damper to match the keyway in the steel crank.

Figure 7.17 This is the stock, 8.1L-style crankshaft sensor at the left rear of the block.

Figure 7.18 and Figure 7.19 The photo on the top shows extreme damage on an X24 count reluctor tooth. The left half of the tooth has been chipped off. The bottom photo shows an X58 count reluctor tooth from the top. Note that the tooth on the right also has a piece missing out of it. This was probably caused by dropping the crank on a steel work bench.

Figure 7.20 If you're going to degree your camshaft, this is the correct type of gear to use. The crankshaft gear is for the Gen 5 and 6 timing chain set—either double or single row. You can tell by the inside keyways on the gear shown (square, diamond, or round) which way the gear is installed. Check the gear back spacing for alignment. There are also lower gears with nine keyways. What usually happens, though, is you keep the stock upper camshaft gear and replace the chain. Factory gears seldom wear, so there's little question the camshaft gear will not be read by the sensor. Aftermarket camshaft gears occasionally present problems for the computer. So, if possible, keep the stock upper gear.

Figure 7.21 You can see how the above-mentioned crankshaft gear works with the 2004 and up, X1, double row chain and sprocket.

Figure 7.22, Figure 7.23, Figure 7.24, Figure 7.25, Figure 7.26 These five combined photos represent work that Larry did 15 years ago to design, change, or improve reluctors that could be installed inside the front timing cover.

Figure 7.27 If you have the patience and skill required, this is what wiring a computer can look like. The computer itself is the small grey box at the bottom of the illustration.

Figure 7.28 This is a prototype piece which allows 8.1L timing reluctors to be pressed onto a Gen 5 or Gen 6 one-piece rear main seal crankshaft.

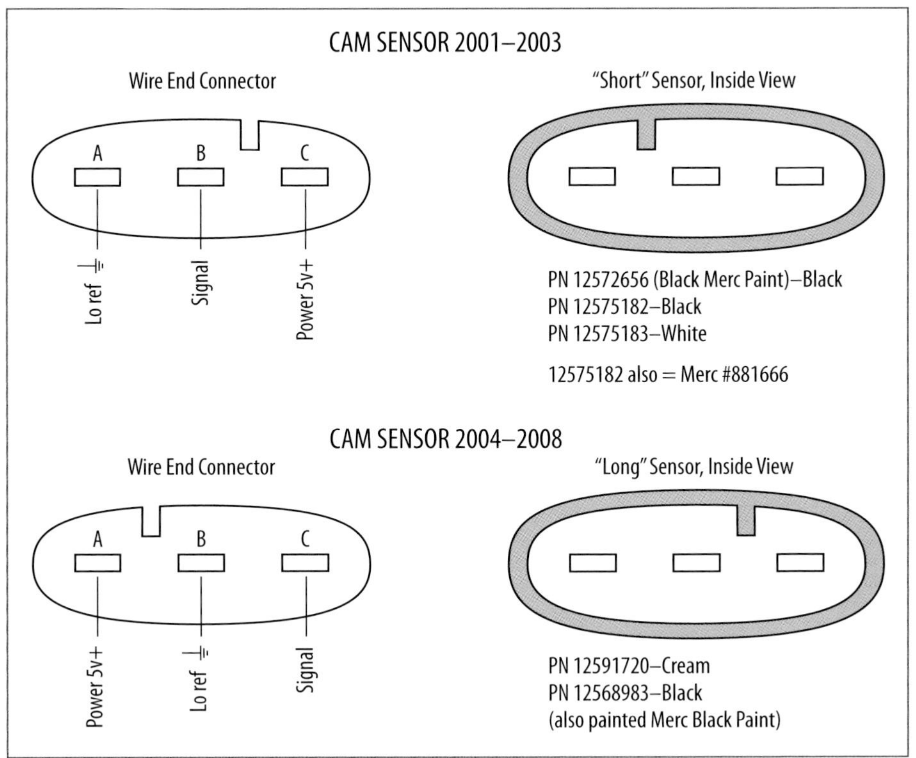

Figure 7.29 Cam sensor wiring diagram.

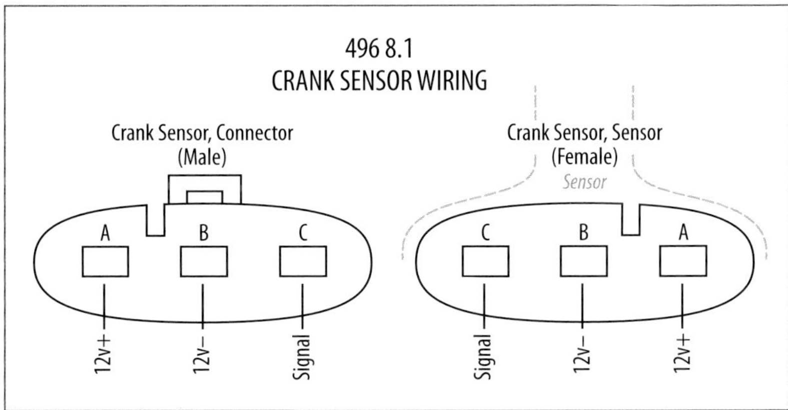

Figure 7.30 Crankshaft sensor wiring diagram.

8

Cooling Systems

There is one simple system in the development of this book that we did not want to overlook: the cooling system. It seems simple at first—radiator, thermostat, water pump, and hoses for the water to run through. However, today the system is much more sophisticated. Engines are running hotter and generating more power, so engineers had to design better ways to control the heat through the engine.

Background

One of the advantages of the new 8.1L over the Gen 4, 5, and 6 big blocks was the redesign of the heads to include symmetrical ports and increase water core size, volume, and routing of the water inside the heads. In doing this, the volume and flow of water inside the heads was increased which eliminated hotspots around the exhaust ports and spark plugs. This was considered a necessary improvement as there were always cooling problems with the Gen 4, 5, and 6 big-block engines.

One of the most obvious external changes for the 8.1L was rerouting the water leaving the engine through a water crossover out of the front of the heads, instead of through the intake manifold as in the Gen 4, 5, and 6. (Smokey Yunick developed this design for the GM small-block in the mid '60s.) This redesign accomplished two things. First, it kept heat out of the intake manifold which in turn kept the airflow cooler. With cooler intake airflow, more timing advance was allowed in the computer tuning process thus producing more power. Second, per the wisdom of Paul Murphy at Murph's Speedboat Shop, it allowed a higher volume of water flow through the block and heads for improved thermal control, allowing the engine to run leaner to control emissions.

Trucks with the 8.1L use a larger radiator than the same truck using the smaller LS version engine. The radiator core in the 8.1L engine is 38" wide, 21" high, and 2.50" thick. This large radiator was designed to handle the total possible BTUs produced by a stock, 8.1L engine.

GM has given lots of additional cooling capacity to trucks for most applications. As an example, the 8.1L installed in Larry's 2000 Corvette uses the stock GM 5.7L radiator, 26" wide, 17" tall and 1.50" thick with stock cooling fans installed from the factory. With the A/C running, it can sit for an hour and maintain a temperature of 190°F. General Motors did a good job developing the cooling system for the 8.1L.

For the 2001 to 2005 trucks, GM has a large thermostatically controlled engine-driven fan to pull air through the radiator and A/C condenser. It works well but makes lots of noise and consumes a fair amount of horsepower when fully engaged. Sometimes when idling, there would not be enough air flow through the A/C condenser, and the A/C high sideline pressure will increase and shut off the A/C compressor. When air flow increases through the A/C condenser by the vehicle moving again, the high sideline pressure drops, and the compressor turns on again. This makes the passenger compartment cooling unpredictable.

The stock engine radiator, if in good shape, works well and engine temperatures generally operate in the 200–220°F range determined by the 190°F thermostat. The stock radiator has the capacity to cool to a lower temperature if a lower temperature thermostat is installed. The hottest location in the engine is the area between the exhaust ports of the cylinder heads. This is also where the dash temperature gauge sensor is located on the passenger side cylinder head.

For the later LS and 8.1 engines, the engine-driven fan was replaced with electric cooling fans. The engine management computer is used to control when the fans turn on and off. This has made the cooling much less dependent on vehicle speed. This also results in more useable power at the crankshaft. When the vehicle is moving the fans turn off, when the A/C doesn't need the added air flow they turn off, and when it is cold outside, they turn off. The fans are only used when the computer deems necessary. They are also much quieter and easier to service.

The same electric fan system can be retrofitted to 2001 and later trucks. The kits are available on the internet or at auto parts stores. We bought one of these fan kits at O'Reilly Auto Parts and installed it in a 2003 Suburban. It came with the relays and loom for the computer. The stock 8.1 computer has the operating system to run the fans. It needs to be turned on by a computer technician who will also set the temperatures for when the fans should turn on and off.

Water Pumps

Variations with truck engines begin with two different stock water pumps. On the first pump, the water inlet is pointed straight out the passenger side of the engine. The 2500 trucks, Yukons, and Suburbans used this type of water pump. Some 3500 medium-duty trucks and vans also used the pump. (Figure 8.01). We've added the second photo to show how the belt tensioner is attached to the 2500 and 3500 truck models (Figure 8.02). The second type of stock 8.1L water pump has the water inlet pointed straight down on the passenger side and is used on some of the 3500s and the heavy duty 4500 and 5500 trucks (Figure 8.03). The third pump shown is an aluminum, short, big block water pump used on Gen 4, 5, or 6 engines (Figure 8.04). It is used when making custom accessory belt drives. It can be either a long or short pump as the attaching bolt pattern is the same. You can contact any aftermarket company that manufactures serpentine belt drives for a tall deck, big block Chevy, for a custom drive look.

Front Water Crossovers

There are three standard General Motors versions. First, the crossover with the thermostat housing on the driver's side is the most common and is used in the 2500 and 3500 model trucks (Figure 8.05). The second style is the medium- and heavy-duty truck crossover with the thermostat housing in the middle (Figure 8.06). The third type of GM crossover contains the thermostat housing on the passenger's side and is used in heavy-duty trucks and marine applications (Figure 8.07).

Last, is a crossover made for a custom accessory drive where there was interference with the throttle body on a modified stock intake. This would work for a Camaro or Chevelle where it puts the throttle body in conflict with the stock crossover. The one shown in the illustration was made to work with the Gen 4 and 5 aluminum Corvette water pump and a stack fuel injection system (Figure 8.08).

Figure 8.01 Here we have the stock 8.1L water pump used in the 2500 and 3500 series truck line. You will note the water inlet is pointed out to the side.

Figure 8.02 The above photograph illustrates how the belt tensioner is attached to the 2500–3500 series truck water pump.

Figure 8.03 A different pump is used in the 3500–5500-series truck line. The height of the pump is different, and the water inlet is pointed straight down.

Figure 8.04 This is a typical short aluminum big-block, Gen 4, 5, and 6, water pump. It has the same mounting holes as the stock 8.1L water pump.

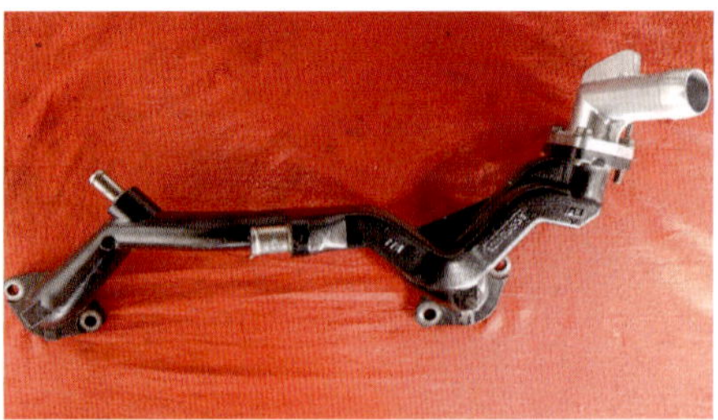

Figure 8.05 The most common water crossover for the 2500–3500-series truck engine.

Figure 8.06 A water crossover from the 3500–5500 truck series.

Figure 8.07 This water crossover is used in some of the heavy-duty truck cooling systems and in the 8.1L marine engine cooling system.

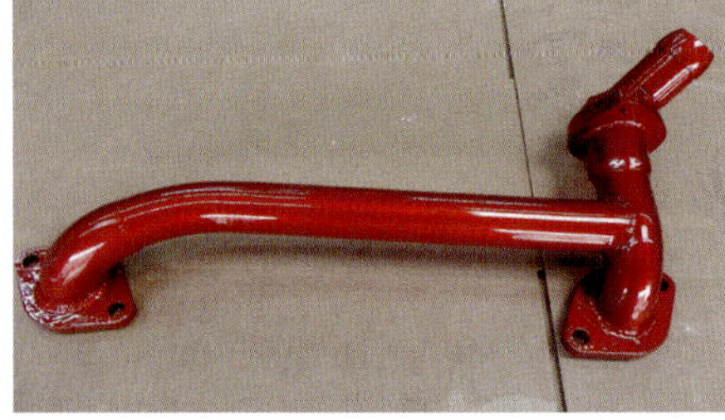

Figure 8.08 At some point you may need to make a custom water crossover. Larry built this one. It is used to clear an intake manifold with the throttle body pointed straight out to the front, similar to a small-block, LS intake manifold.

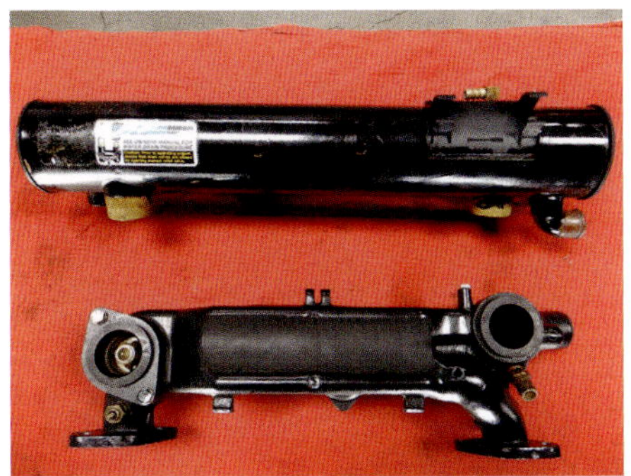

Figure 8.09 If you are working on a marine engine, here is what you will need. This is a Mercury Marine crossover. It includes a water-to-water heat exchanger. It has many tubes inside the cooler that have engine cooling water on the inside of the tubes and raw water flowing over the outside of these tubes, and all of these tubes are included inside the heat exchanger. This is what removes engine heat. This is in essence the marine engine's radiator.

The cooling in a marine closed cooling system is accomplished by pumping water out of the lake or ocean (called raw water) and into and out of the heat exchanger. The stock 496 CID heat exchanger is 3" in diameter. A heavy-duty heat exchanger can be ordered from Sea Kamp Engineering in a 4" diameter for supercharged and higher horsepower engines. Higher horsepower engines produce more BTUs than the stock heat exchanger can remove.

The second water crossover is the heavy-duty GM truck crossover (refer back to Figure 8.07). It is mostly used in marine engines where the engines are raw water cooled. This is where the external water is pumped directly into the engine and back out to cool the exhaust. The disadvantage to this system is that salty water will corrode the inside of the block and heads, and the dirt or sand in the water will fill up the water jackets in the block. Again, you don't have the advantage of antifreeze to keep from corroding aluminum heads and manifolds.

Raw Water Pumps

These two raw water pumps (Figure 8.10) are typical of the marine world. The Mercury (black pump) is used with the closed cooling system on the 375 and 425 hp engines. The silver pump is used with most other marine engines using a non-closed cooling system or raw water cooling system.

This photo shows how a raw water pump works internally. (Figure 8.11). The rubber impeller is turned by a belt from the crankshaft. The water is drawn into the center chamber from the right-side inlet port. The impeller moves the water to the left side of the pump and out the left side port. Working pressure can be as high as 28–32 psi.

Marine 8.1L Crossovers

One of the best improvements in the boating industries has been the advent of the closed cooling system and the use of antifreeze in the marine cooling system. Some manufacturers and race boats still use raw water cooling because of simplicity and reduced weight.

In the marine environment the two most common crossovers are the Mercury Marine used strictly by Mercury Marine, and the GM crossover that is used by Volvo, Marine Power, Crusader and other small suppliers.

The Mercury crossover is a very sophisticated part (Figure 8.09). The crossover itself is made of aluminum to save weight. It also incorporates a second component called a water-to-water heat exchanger for cooling the antifreeze that circulates in the closed cooling system. The advantage of the antifreeze in the cooling system is to eliminate the corrosion that affects aluminum parts in a raw water cooling system. Additionally, it controls the temperature of the cooling water circulating inside the engine as compared to a raw water cooling system which just circulates lake water directly through the engine.

Figure 8.10 These are two examples of marine raw water pumps. The black pump is for Mercury Marine, 8.1L engines. The silver pump is used on many engines with raw water cooling.

Figure 8.11 Typical of the internal workings of a marine raw water pump.

9

Oiling Systems

We come now to what may seem a fairly irrelevant area of information: the oiling system. You put the oil in the top of the engine and change it by taking it out the bottom. If you're driving a brand-new car this is totally correct. If you're having the engine rebuilt in a reputable shop it remains the same. If you're building the engine, well it becomes a different matter. Let's see what that difference is and how the oiling systems work, looking primarily at the 496 CID, Gen 7 block.

General Motors Oiling System

The stock oiling system delivered by GM for the Gen 7 is a very good system and would be hard to improve upon. GM has had more than 40 years of racing and durability testing to develop this oiling system. It's the most reliable and trouble-free system of all the big-block engines GM has built.

It's a relatively simple process—the oil goes from the pump to the oil filter, then to the oil cooler, back into the engine, then to the main oil galley which supplies oil to the main bearings and cam bearings. After it reaches the oil galley it splits off in the rear to the two additional galleys that supply oil to the lifters and rocker arms. As a note, the GM lifters are of a full-length skirt design. This is required to keep from uncovering the lifter oil galleys when the lifter is at full lift. If aftermarket lifters are used without this skirt, the galleys will be uncovered with the result being low oil pressure.

GM has tried different oil pumps, filters, oil galley arrangements, windage trays, oil cooler, and oil pan configurations. All of this just to make a production Gen 7 big-block engine for anyone, and it will work as expected.

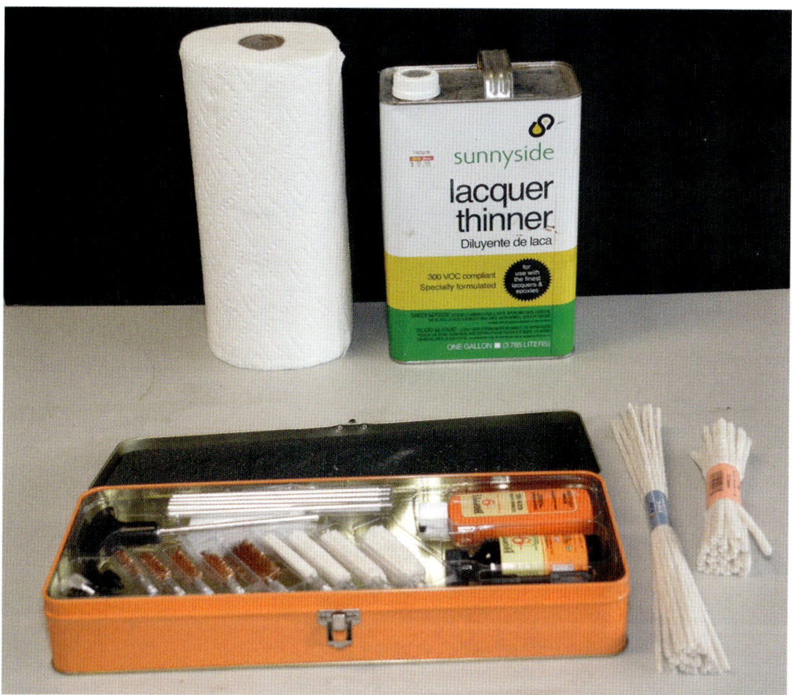

Figure 9.01 Consider this to be the basic oil systems cleaning ensemble: a gun cleaning kit for all caliber sizes, pipe cleaners, some enamel or lacquer solvent, and a roll of paper towels. You may want to add a dowel as a push stick or a roll of mechanics wire to pull the paper towels through.

Engine Cleaning

When a piece of dirt or grime gets into the engine through the oiling system, then there is a tendency for that grime to cause a blockage in the system. The pump can't take in enough oil to pump oil back out, then your engine can't get enough oil and it seizes, resulting in a dead engine.

Factory-built engines are well cleaned as they're manufactured. If you buy a new short-block engine from a reputable dealer, you'll have no problem. When you break down the engine and send it out, the problems usually begin. When your block comes back it's your responsibility to see that it's thoroughly cleaned. Here is how to do it.

We went out and bought a top-quality gun cleaning kit, two types of pipe cleaners, some paint thinner (lacquer), and a big roll of paper towels—cloth doesn't work well because it leaves lint. (Figure 9.01)

Begin by inspecting all the oil galleys. Attach a brush of proper size to the handle and go to work. As you go through

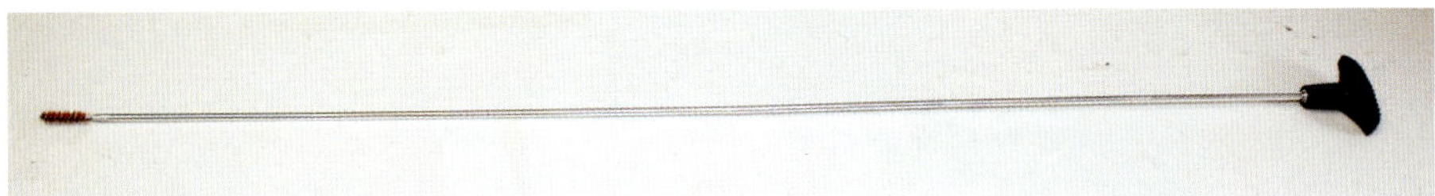

Figure 9.02 To show you how this works for a long bore, we've screwed six extensions (found in the kit) together and added a brush to the end.

the galleys the sizes will be different, so you'll have to change brush sizes (Figure 9.02). Next come the pipe cleaners for each galley. Soak a pipe cleaner in paint thinner or lacquer thinner and pass it through the galley. For the larger galleys use a paper towel soaked in thinner and pushed through with a stick or pulled through with a wire. From here, wash everything with Tide or Dawn dish soap and lots of warm water. When that is done, blow the engine and parts dry so the clean metal doesn't rust. It's your responsibility to make the engine clean! (For further info on cleaning your engine, see *How to Rebuild Small-Block Mopar Engines* by yours truly, Don Taylor and Larry Hofer, published by HP Books). Now that you have a very clean engine, let's look at the parts of the oiling system.

Figure 9.03 A stock oil pump mounted to a 496 CID 8.1L engine.

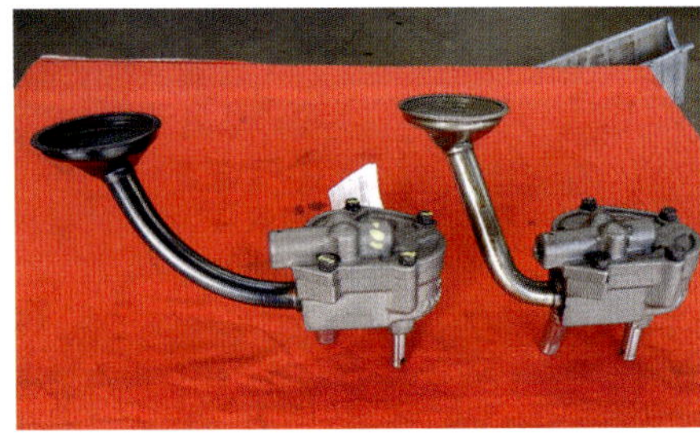

Figure 9.04 On the left we have a high-volume pump with a marine or industrial pick-up; on the right is a stock volume, 8.1L pump and its pick-up. From all outward appearances they look the same; inside they're different.

Oil Pump

The GM oil pump has been sized to work with the production bearing clearances of a new block. (Figure 9.03) (Figure 9.04) With these tighter bearing clearances you can use a pump of less volume and this in turn requires less horsepower to turn the pump. This is GM's take on things: less parasitic drag equals more useable horsepower. In a production Gen 7, with the oil temperature at 180°F, it's still within GM specifications to see 15 lbs oil pressure at 650 rpm. The oil pressure should increase to 40–45 psi as soon as the engine rpm is increased to 2000 rpm. The tighter clearances in a new production short block work fine with the smaller volume pump. However, if you're assembling a performance engine, the bearing clearance will be increased to the maximum production limits. This is a part of the blue printing system and is usually determined by the person or shop that's building your engine. (For further discussions on blue printing see the chapter on big-block assembly.)

The stock Gen 7 oil pump rotors are 1.140" tall and are driven by the oil pump drive shaft. The pump uses a ¾" oil pick-up tube. It also has increased clearance designed into the underside of the pump housing for the increased crank shaft counterweight clearance.

Pump Disassembly

If you feel your oil pump may be causing problems, it can be taken apart and checked for excess clearance between the rotors and end plate with a maximum clearance of .0025". Make sure foreign debris has not gone through the rotors. You don't want to see any scarring. While the cover is off the pump, remove the roll pin that holds in the relief-valve spring. Take out the pressure relief valve of the pump cover. If it is binding or sticking, find out why. If it has score marks inside, your best choice is to get a new pump because the valve assembly probably has metal particles binding it. When reassembling, use Loctite and torque the cover bolts to 110–120 in-lbs.

Melling High-Volume Oil Pump

Many 8.1L engine builders use a high-volume oil pump because it produces higher oil pressure at idle and lower engine speeds. The Melling High Volume Oil Pump (HV 10778C) has taller rotors (1.400") and also uses a ¾" oil pick-up tube. This pump will produce higher oil pressure at idle and lower engine speeds, as mentioned before. This is useful if your engine builder has opened up the clearances of your rotating assembly. Most high-volume oil pumps start to bypass oil at the pump at about 2500–3000 rpm so there is a tradeoff. The downside for the high-volume oil pump is that it also requires as much as 10 hp to drive the pump at 6000 rpm!

For comparison though, an engine with .002–.0025" bearing clearances will show 40 psi with cold oil, and 20 psi at 900 rpm with warm, 180-degree oil. Switching to a Melling High Volume pump will bring the oil pressure up to 60 psi cold, and 40 psi at 900 rpm with 180°F oil temp.

How It All Works

The Gen 7 oil pump drive is driven off the gear on the rear of the cam. (Figure 9.05) This gear drives either a distributor as in early GM engines, or the oil pump drive, such as the '92–'96 LT1 small-blocks or the Gen 7. The oil pump itself is driven by the oil pump drive shaft between the bottom of the stub drive and the main shaft into the oil pump. (Figure 9.06) The oil pump-to-block bolt torque is 56–60 ft-lbs.

In the Gen 7 block, there are two oil bypass valves. One, in case the oil filter gets plugged and another if the oil cooler gets plugged. Both of these valves are designed to allow the oil to go directly back into the main oiling

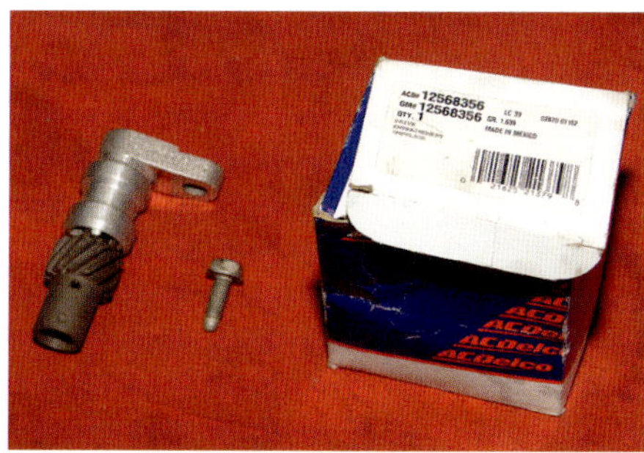

Figure 9.05 This is the 8.1L oil pump drive assembly. It's driven by the cam gear and couples to the oil pump drive shaft.

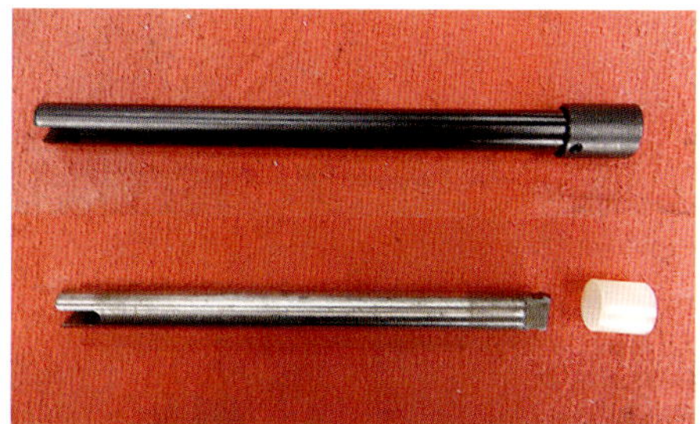

Figure 9.06 The black oil pump drive shaft at the top of the photo is a heavy-duty shaft with a steel coupler. The lower bronze colored shaft is a stock drive with a stock plastic coupler.

Figure 9.07 Here are the locations of the in and out oil cooler ports.

Figure 9.08 This picture tells us a lot. This is a 572 CID, 8.1L engine showing where the oil pump mounts in the rear. In the center of the oil filter mounting plate you can see down the hole to the check valve for the oil cooler. Finally, note the X58 count timing reluctor at the rear of the engine. In stock engines this would have been an X24 count reluctor.

Figure 9.09 We have here a stock, Mercury marine engine with its oil cooler (painted red) mounted to the side. The first thing to note is that there is no oil filter on the bottom of the engine. How would you change it in a boat? Note that it has a plate with a hose. Oil comes out of the black filter cover and goes to a remote filter located on the front of the engine. It then comes down to the rear of the oil cooler, through the cooler, and then returns to the block. The Dart block was not developed with these bolt bosses to mount the cooler. Therefore, if you're using a Dart block, you'll have to use your imagination on how and where to mount the cooler. General Motors, World Products, and PSI all have these extra bosses cast into the block.

system bypassing the plugged component. (Figure 9.07) (Unfortunately, by then it is too late for your bearings!)

There are also two different bypass spring pressures. One for the truck world which has a relief pressure of 15 psi. (PN 25013765). The second one is for the marine world and has a relief pressure of 30 psi. (PN 25161284). Both of these bypass valves are located in the oil filter pad. (Figure 9.08) One is under the threaded insert in the center of the oil filter pad, and the other is on the block surface. Both of these check valves should be removed during the cleaning process to remove any particles trapped in the oil galleys under the valves.

For those who need to modify their oil pump or have a need for a more specialized oil pump, David Vizard's book, *Chevy Big-Blocks, Max Performance*, deals with this in depth.

Figure 9.10 These are ½" pipe fitting to #10 AN (Army/Navy) fittings for making custom oil cool connections. Army/Navy fittings are derived from joint military standards and date back to WWII.

Figure 9.11 These are factory truck oil connectors and lines to the oil cooler. The one closest to the bottom is the oil return and the one at the top is the oil supply to the cooler.

Oil Coolers

GM has included oil cooler connections in the Gen 7 block, and, they are used in all OEM installations. Oil temperature control is extremely important in trucks, marine, and race engines. (Figure 9.09) Keeping the oil temperature under control is good for oil life and keeps it from breaking down under extreme loads and heat. GM's recommendation for oil temperature is 200 to 250°F, but in the marine world 160 to 200°F is more in line. Anything above 250°F begins to break down the oil and 270°F will cause the bearings to overheat. In the automotive world there is also some horsepower to be found by running the oil temp high. At higher temperatures, the oil thins out and reduces the parasitic horsepower losses.

In stock applications, these oil cooler connections at the oil pan rail are connected to the coolers, either in the truck radiator or a marine heat exchanger. These coolers work extremely well and maintain the oil temperature within the desired temperature range. This is also part of the reason these engines can be disassembled after being run for thousands of miles and the bearings look perfect. This cooler should always be included in new construction projects. For these projects it is easy to get two ½" NP by #10 AN fittings (Figure 9.10) to connect into the oil cooler ports at the block and fabricate oil cooler lines to an external Earl's-style oil cooler, or a cooler from a Heavy Duty 4500 and bigger truck that has the add-on oil coolers. These should be mounted where there is good airflow. The usual place would be in front of the radiator. Use only #10 hose and fittings or bigger.

We've seen engines where the oil cooler ports were simply plugged and now have low oil pressure. The reason for this is the oil pump must push all the oil through the oil relief check valve which has a tiny ⅜" hole for the oil to go through (Figure 9.11). Hook up the oil cooler! Some less known marine engine companies just fashion a loop of hose and hook the outgoing oil port to the incoming oil port and call it good. This doesn't work well—it gives up the benefit of having cooled engine oil. Remember: you would like to have the oil between 180 and 220°F. When you see 250 to 260°F it's time to get off the throttle and let the oil cool down. If the engine you're rebuilding has had a terminal failure, it's best to replace the oil cooler or radiator with a new one. You don't want to take a chance of bearing material making its way into the new engine! Before we move on to oil pans, let's look at some clearances from a 2004 Truck Service Manual.

General Motors Recommended Engine Bearing Clearances

2004 Truck Service Manual	*Minimum Clearance*	*Maximum Clearance*
Connecting Rod Side Clearances	.015"	.027"
Connecting Rod Clearances	.0013"	.0027"
Main Bearing Clearances	.0013"	.0027"
Crank End Play	.005"	.014"

The minimum clearance specifications would be considered tight and used in a stock rebuild. The maximum limit specifications would be looser so therefore used in a performance engine. The machine shop assembler will help you make the decision on what clearances to use.

Oil Pans

We turn our attention now to the oil pan. Selecting the right oil pan for the engine is very important. Unfortunately, there are few stock choices. We'll try to help you select the correct pan for the engine you're developing.

When the Gen 7 engine was developed, GM made a pan that was specific to the Gen 7 block. For instance, the oil pan rail on the block is wider than a Gen 4, 5, or 6. This means that only an oil pan designed to fit on a Gen 7 block will work. The front timing cover radius is the same as a Gen 5 and 6, but the 5 and 6 pan seal area across the timing cover is a female O-ring gasket groove and not flat as in the Gen 7. The rear main cap seal radius for a Gen 5 and 6 is different than a Gen 7 rear main cap seal. So, there is no interchangeability between the Gen 5 and 6 oil pan and the Gen 7 pan.

The Gen 7 oil pans are cast aluminum for all applications with the exception of a company called Dooley Enterprises that make specialty oil pans

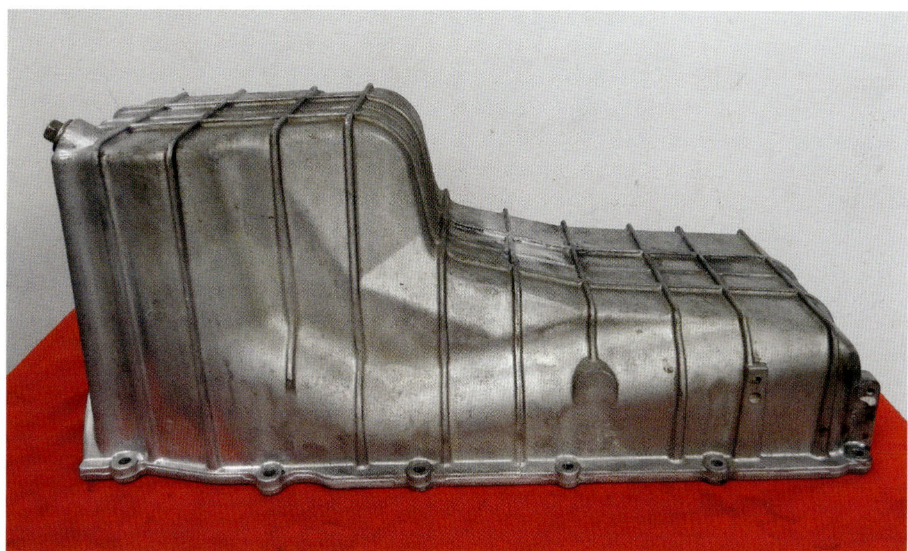

Figure 9.12 Trucks are a major part of the industry. Here, we have an 8.1L, cast aluminum truck pan.

Figure 9.15 These are the dipstick-to-pan fittings and the dipstick tube. These fittings are for the marine and industrial pans. Obviously, when the dipstick hits that 90-degree turn it stops.

Figure 9.13 These two pick-ups serve two different purposes. The one on the left is a marine pick-up working in a deep pan—while the other could be used if you cut the bottom off an 8.1L truck pan to gain road clearance. The one on the right serves custom pan builders.

for the marine industry. Dooley's pans are half cast-aluminum and half sheet metal. For further information on these pans checkout Dooley Enterprises.

Truck Oil Pans

The stock GM 8 qt oil pan for trucks is the one that's most available, as it was on all 8.1L trucks from 2001 to 2008 (Figure 9.12). This oil pan also lends itself quite well to modifications for use in all the GM A-bodies (Chevelle, GTO, Buick, and Oldsmobile) and F-bodies (Camaro, Firebird).

The 8.1L truck oil pan is made of good, weldable aluminum. Aluminum pans need to be welded by tungsten inert gas (TIG welding). Usually, the front shallow section of the pan will clear the front cross member depending on the motor mounts used. The main concern though, is the sump hanging below the cross member causing possible road damage. If you're going to use this pan, the depth will need to be determined by fitting the block and pan into the chassis. Road clearance here is important.

Think of this: when a cast aluminum pan hits an object while driving, it doesn't cause a leak, it simply explodes and dumps all the oil instantly. This is obviously not a good thing. It's very important to work on ground

Figure 9.16 The three plugs you see next to the camshaft retainer are factory 496 cam galley plugs. They are drilled with .060 bleed holes. These holes do two things. They bleed air out of the oiling system on startup very quickly and keep the lifters from getting air into them and clicking till the air is displaced. Also, they oil the timing chain and gears. In this photo, you can see tiny holes in each plug. Some shops prefer to block off these bleeds.

Figure 9.14 A stock marine or industrial 10 qt oil pan ready to bolt on. The silver bolt bore is where the dipstick tube will go.

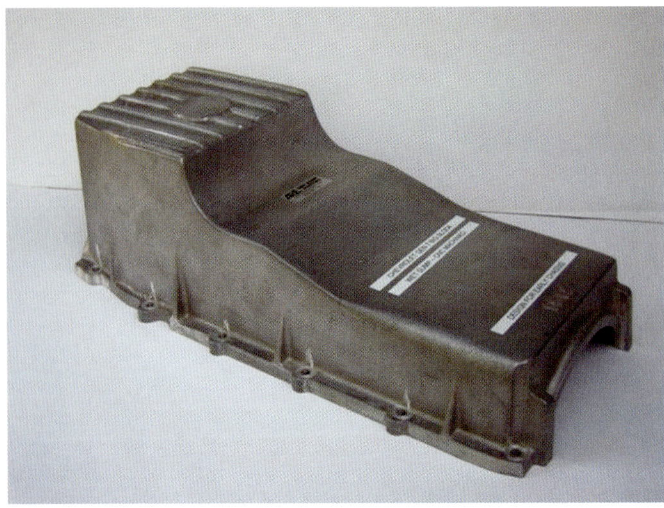

Figure 9.17 This oil pan was commissioned by Chevrolet to be made by ARE Dry Sump Systems for the Gen 7 in 2003. They are presently being recast by ARE for installation in Gen 7 passenger cars.

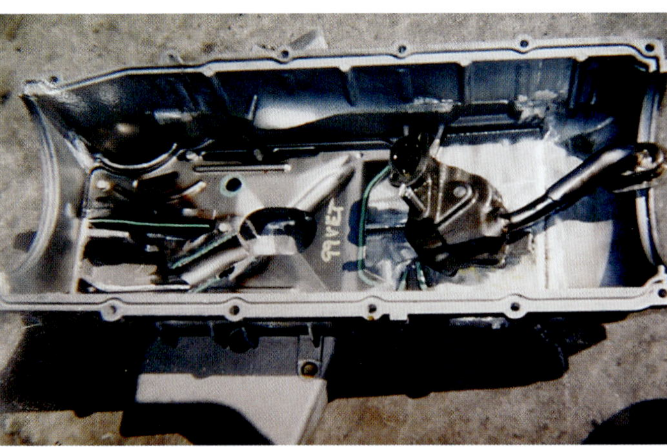

Figure 9.18 Larry insisted we publish this picture. The top is an 8.1L truck oil pan, grafted to a 1999 Corvette oil pan bottom. It was made to install in a Corvette of that year. Both pans were aluminum and lent themselves to this kind of modification. Note the oil pump is a stock, low-volume 8.1L with an LS1 oil pick-up. Larry says it's still in operation.

clearance issues to avoid this type of disaster. Just imagine a hot rod with an expensive engine and air ride suspension. This would be an unimaginable disaster! The usual modification is to cut off the lower sump of the pan by 2 or 3" for good ground clearance and then have a good welder reattach a bottom. Shorten the oil pump pickup to match or locate a big-block 427 corvette oil pick up and you'll have a great combination (Figure 9.13).

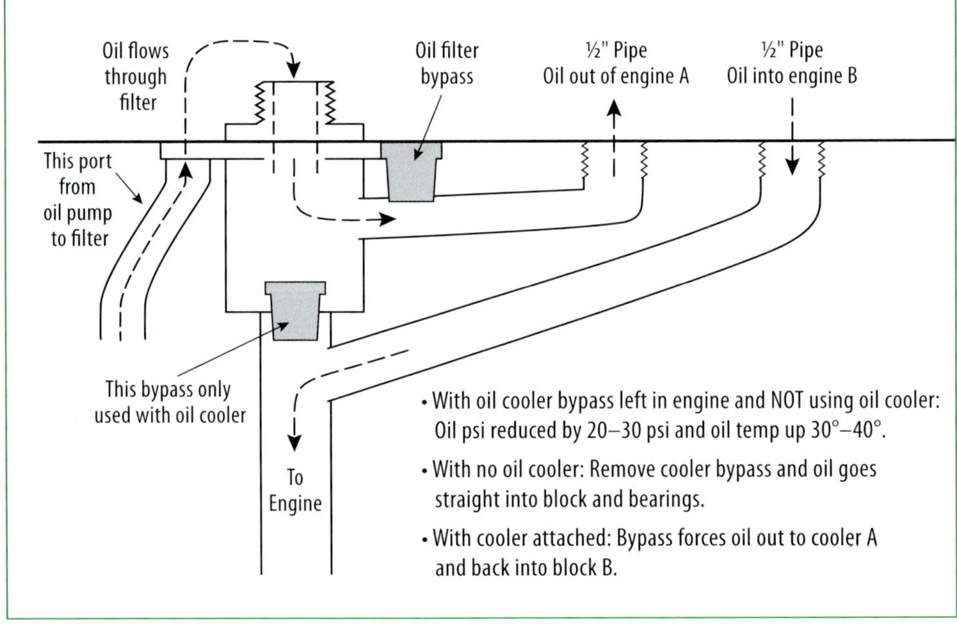

Figure 9.19 This diagram shows how the oil bypass system works.

Marine and Industrial Applications

The GM marine and industrial oil pan is a full length, deep oil pan and holds 10 qts. It works well in both marine and industrial applications. There's really not much that can be done with this oil pan (Figures 9.14, 9.15, and 9.16)

Car Pans

In 2002, General Motors commissioned ARE Dry Sump Systems to make a passenger car oil pan for the 8.1L engine and offer it in the GM Performance Parts catalogue. This pan is now being remanufactured by ARE. For the person interested in a Gen 7 dry sump system, contact www.drysump.com. (Figures 9.17 and 9.18).

10

Big-Block Assembly

In this chapter we begin the big block assembly with a new, 8.1L-style short block. Please don't get confused between the short block and small block. The short block is the lower portion of the engine with the rotating assembly installed (pistons, rods, and crankshaft). Engine displacement has nothing to do with it.

Head Installation

This particular short block is a 4.500 bore and a 4.500 stroke prototype block from World Products and is being assembled for testing. Larry has set the two aluminum heads on the block with the head gaskets in place (Figure 10.01). These high-performance gaskets are called *multi-layer stainless* (MLS) (Figure 10.02). In addition to being "bullet proof," the thickness of the gasket can be made thicker or thinner by adding or subtracting layers in the center. This gives the mechanic the added benefit of being able to make compression adjustments. These gaskets are quite unlike the older composition gaskets. Those consisted of a paper-like (composition) material sandwiched together, and a stainless-steel beading was formed around the edges of the combustion chambers. They were current technology for their day.

Before installing your heads check your gaskets for the correct orientation (Figure 10.03). The gasket in the photograph was laid on backwards, on purpose, to show the difference between the gasket holes and the water ports in the block. *Be sure all the holes line up properly!*

Figure 10.01 Always, always, test what you're doing! It's going to make your work so much easier in the long run than having to tear down what you've done and repair it. Larry is testing to be sure the gaskets are the correct ones for the engine.

Figure 10.02 These MLS gaskets are the next step up in the head gasket line. They're made by adding or deleting layers in the center so that the mechanic can order the exact thickness needed. These are stainless steel.

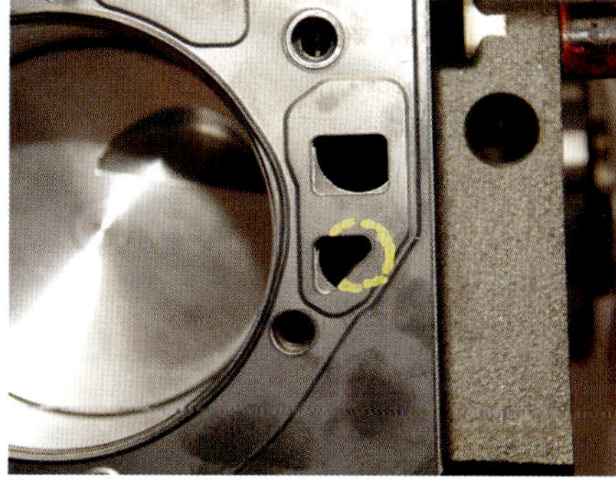

Figure 10.03 We've made an extreme close-up here to show exactly what the head gaskets look like when installed in the correct direction.

Figure 10.04 Larry puts a dab of gasket sealer on the threads of each head bolt. It prevents the bolt from galling and seals the threads so there are no leaks.

Figure 10.05 Working in a clockwise circle while tightening the head bolts prevents warpage between the head and block. Likewise, torquing to three different levels (as described in the text), further prevents this warpage.

With all the holes aligned, you can now begin torqueing the head bolts. Larry uses GM gasket sealer (PN1050026) on all the head bolts (Figure 10.04). This serves two purposes. One, it acts as a lubricant, and second, when this material dries it seals the bolt in its hole and prevents it from leaking coolant. It's a pretty good deal.

Larry has a certain way he torques the bolts which gives him complete assurance the bolts are tightened correctly (Figure 10.05). He begins with the center bolt in the head, tightening it to about 65 percent of the torque value. He then works in a clockwise manner until all the bolts are set. The second time, he tightens everything to about 90–95 percent. The third and final trip brings the reading up to its full, 100 percent torque (Figure 10.06). If you're working with an iron head, the torque value is 60 ft-lbs for the short bolts and 65 ft-lbs for the long bolts. If you're using the aluminum heads, there are two torque values: 50 ft-lbs for the short bolts and 55 ft-lbs for the long bolts. The final step is to install the two freeze plugs in the rear holes of the aluminum heads using 1-⅜" freeze plugs (Figure 10.07). Now, the heads are installed on the block and we're ready for the next step. (Iron heads don't use freeze plugs.)

Figure 10.06 The heads are finished, and all tightened down. Each bolt was tightened three times until all the torque settings were correct.

Camshaft Installation

It's now time to install the camshaft (Figure 10.08). To give you some extra leverage and control, screw a long, 8 mm threaded bolt into the front of the cam (Figure 10.09). You don't want to gouge the cam bearings. Lube the cam journals and lobes with assembly oil and carefully install the cam. When the cam is in, we can place the retainer plate over the front of it. Insert the two torx-head screws using Loctite on the threads (Figure 10.10). Torque to 106 in-lbs. With this quick bit, we can now move on to the timing chain.

Larry has decided to use the double link chain for two reasons: first there's going to be a lot of stress on this engine and we don't want to break a chain. The second reason is that this has an

Figure 10.07 These 1-⅜" freeze plugs are placed in the rear of the heads. Should you place them in the front, you'll find yourself taking them out again because the crossover pipe fastens over these two holes in the front.

Figure 10.08 Larry inserts the camshaft. Be sure to lube all parts to make sure you don't bend, spindle, or mutilate any piece!

Figure 10.09 The long, 8-mm threaded bolt in the camshaft. This helps you get the cam in place.

Figure 10.10 The camshaft retainer plate is fastened to the block. Be sure to use Loctite on the threads and torque to 106-in. lbs.

X4 camshaft sensor top cam gear from GM. This will allow the cam sensor to work with an E38 computer in a 2010 truck.

To install this chain, you must have the camshaft and crankshaft properly aligned. Begin by installing the cam gear onto the camshaft with no chain. Place the dot on the edge of the gear into the straight down position. Turn the crankshaft and gear until the dot is in the straight up position. To confirm this position, line a straight edge up on the two dots. The straight edge should be straight up and down. These two dots *must* line up! (Figure 10.11).

Carefully remove the upper (cam) gear. Install the chain around the top of the gear, keeping the dot straight down. Now slip the timing chain under the crankshaft gear, trying to keep the two dots matched. If you did it correctly the cam gear will align perfectly with the three bolt holes on the camshaft. If you missed it by one or two gear teeth, remove the gear from the cam, drop it down, and rotate it left or right accordingly. Replace the gear onto the cam and everything should be just perfect. Using Loctite, torque the three timing gear bolts down to 22 ft-lbs. Now, it's time to install the timing cover. Let's finish this off.

Figure 10.11 Here we have the cam gear and the crankshaft gear aligned. You can see the two dots line up perfectly. Originally, these were stamped markings. We put the yellow paint on them to make them identifiable by the reader.

Figure 10.12 The seal is pressed in about halfway working from the bottom up. Now, add a dollop of silicone into the channels where the seal bends outwards.

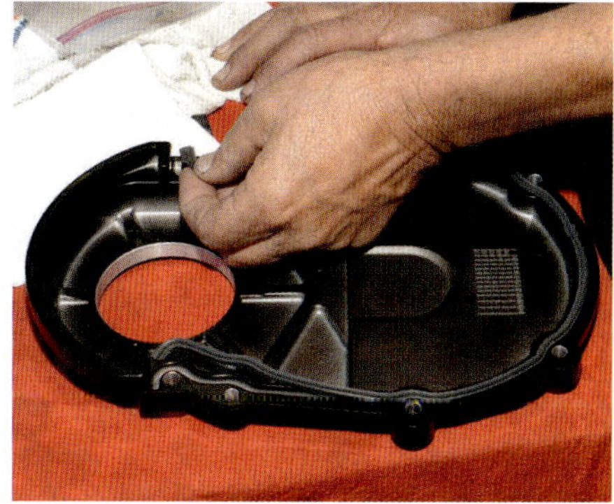

Figure 10.13 Larry begins inserting the seal at the middle, working his way up on each side.

In your kit of gaskets, you'll find one that looks like the one in the illustration. The ends are even bent for you (Figure 10.12). There is also a large lip seal (crankshaft seal) for the front cover. This needs to be tapped into the cover with the lip inboard. Center the gasket at the bottom with the ridge side up (Figure 10.13). Adjust the gasket until the bent ends are in the bends of the cover, then push the gasket in tight, all but the two bent ends. Place a bit of silicone in the end slots then push the gasket down into it. Align the two dowels with their proper two holes in the cover.

Bolt the cover over the timing gear and chain and torque the bolts to 106 in-lbs. Larry likes to write on the timing cover what's behind it so he doesn't forget (Figure 10.32). What those initials mean to Larry is: BP 207 is the camshaft I.D. X4 gear is the camshaft pulses, per revolution, sent to the computer. The standard camshaft sensor reads one pulse per revolution.

Installing the Lifters

To install the lifters, begin by dipping each individual hydraulic roller lifter in oil. As each set of lifters is installed, place one of the "dog bones" (lifter retainer guide) over them (Figure 10.14). After all sixteen lifters are installed we have another part called "the spider." Instead, let's call it the lifter-retainer (Figure 10.15), and it is held in with four bolts. This looks like an excellent solution and is. It works well with almost all applications, but here comes the disclaimer.

In the marine application we've seen instances of the intake manifold valley tray being knocked out of its correct location through heavy impact loading. This in turn, allows the valley tray to rattle around in the lifter valley. The computer knock sensors can register this sound and shut down the engine. The computer doesn't know whether this is the valley tray banging around, a spun rod bearing, or a broken rocker arm. Now, here's a quick story.

Larry sponsored a big rough water race boat, which failed after about half an hour. When they brought it back to the shop, they discovered that with all the banging and thrashing these boats take, the intake valley tray had come loose, and was in fact banging around in the lifter valley. You can imagine the disaster. What was the solution? He put a spacer under each end bolt holding the lifter retainer in place. The bolt touches the lifter valley tray from the bottom (as above) and now the tray cannot drop down into the valley. Therefore, there's no thrashing of the tray and it stays firmly in place (Figure 10.16). The following month the same boat won in its class. If you're building your engine for marine use, remember this: don't forget the spacer under the two end bolts holding the valley tray.

When prepping for installing the intake gaskets, there are four tabs protruding from the head gaskets—one at each corner. Use a pair of pliers to bend these tabs down so they don't interfere with installing the intake manifold (Figure 10.17). Let's move on to getting the pushrods installed.

Figure 10.14 These are the "dog bones" referred to in the body of the chapter. They hold the lifters in place.

Figure 10.15 The lifter-retainer (the spider) has been installed. Each leg holds down a lifter-retainer guide.

Figure 10.16 This is an important "fix" to prevent the damages noted in the text, and it works really well.

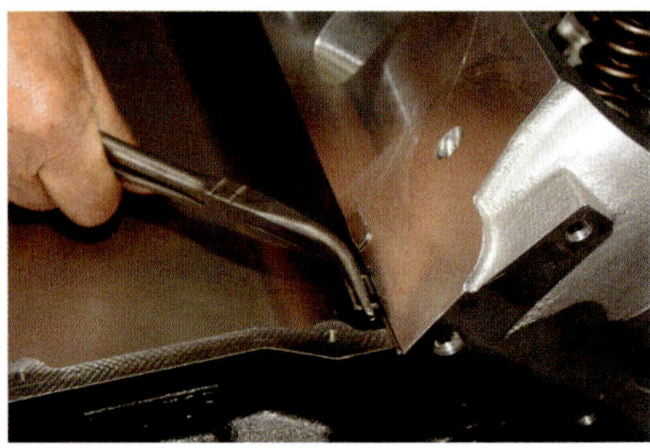

Figure 10.17 At each corner edge of the head gasket are tabs with a slot in them. These tabs must be bent down. The intake manifold gasket has a prong at each end of the bottom that fit in those slots.

Pushrods

Stock, OEM, pushrods are what we're going to use in this application. Now, there are those of you reading this book who will say, “Whoa, I don't think so. My mechanic says aftermarket pushrods are superior.” Well, let's clarify our reasoning. Yes, aftermarket suppliers sell excellent pushrods, but they may not be necessary for what you're building. If you're using a cam of conservative lift (.480–.520) and a standard base circle diameter, you can use your stock pushrods and they'll work fine. If you're building an engine with a cam of more duration and lift, with a smaller base circle, you'll need to use a longer pushrod to keep the non-adjustable rocker geometry correct. Be sure to measure this pushrod length. Generally, .060 will get you back in the working range. Also, there's an opinion that the aftermarket pushrods are stiffer, and you might see a slight increase in hp at higher rpms due to the stiffer pushrods. Crower, Crane, COMP Cams, and others, all sell fine parts. Use what you and your mechanic think best.

Rocker Arms

In the past, some angry problems have arisen with stock rocker arms within the operating environment of the marine and high-performance engines. We have occasionally seen similar problems in truck and industrial applications.

Generally, with truck and industrial engines, the stock rocker arms seem to do well. The stock, GM stamped rocker arms were improved over the 454 and 502 rockers with the addition of an oil deflector over the pushrod oil hole (Figure 10.18). This deflector directed the oil spray from the pushrods directly onto the rocker trunnion balls. This improved the durability of these rockers but didn't eliminate the basic problem: friction and heat generated by the ball in the seat of the rocker. At high rpms and spring loads, this increased friction produces heat causing the rocker arm seat to turn purple and black, thereby weakening the rocker (Figure 10.19).

Aftermarket roller rocker arms eliminate this source of friction and heat by putting needle roller bearings in the pivot point of the rocker. These bearings roll back and forth instead of sliding on two surfaces. In addition to being more durable, this reduction in friction increases the horsepower on the dynamometer by 16 to 18 hp. It also reduces the oil temperature by 20°F.

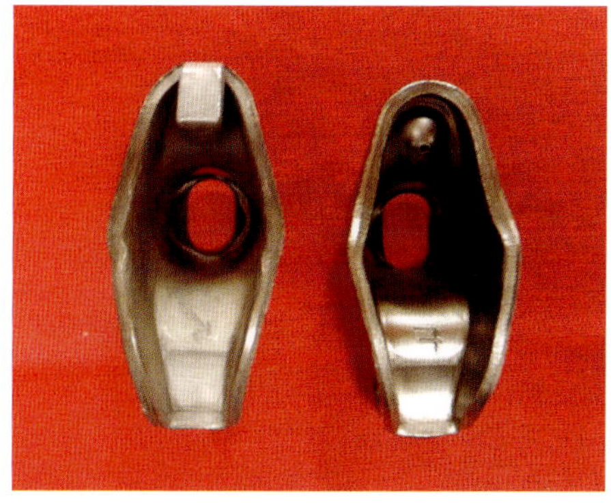

Figure 10.18 Here is a comparison of the two types of rocker arms. On the right is the "old fashioned" rocker with no deflection attachment. The left one has the deflection shield attached.

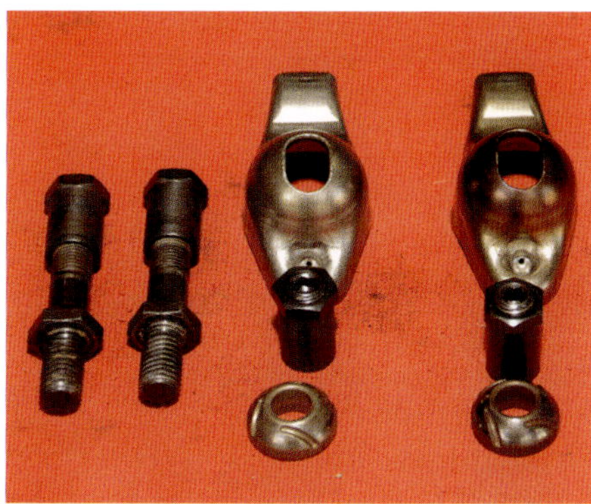

Figure 10.19 The rocker arm at the right of this photo has been over-heated. This causes the metal to turn purple then black, which leads to part failure.

The next issue with roller rockers is how they are made. There are cast stainless steel (Figure 10.20) and billet aluminum rockers (Figure 10.21) available for the 496 8.1L. The stainless-steel rockers are a little more petite in size and don't interfere with, or contact any point, in the head. The aluminum rockers, being softer metal, require more mass to be as strong as the stainless rockers, and therefore are larger in design. They also have an issue with hitting the back valve cover rail and need to be adjusted for clearance to fit. If you're building an engine in your garage, we'd suggest you use the stainless-steel rocker in order to eliminate the machinist's work to resize each rocker arm. Overall, though, both types of rockers work well.

Figure 10.20 Here are three stainless rocker arms. The one on the left is the most important. It shows the flat side of the trunnion facing up. This is the side of the trunnion you want in the up position as you install it. The trunnion in the middle is on the opposite side and faces down. The last trunnion has the nut sitting on top of the flat surface to show that there is nothing extending above the rocker arm.

Figure 10.21 This is an example of an aluminum rocker arm. You can see how much more clearance is required to fit this type of rocker inside the valve covers.

There are two ways to install roller rockers. First, you can buy ARP rocker studs with $\frac{7}{16}$" shanks and 10 mm threads that fit into the head (part #135-7221). You can also use the poly locks (part #300-8242) and buy a set of roller rocker arms. This combination works quite well when it comes to adjusting the valve train. But, as usual, there are problems with this application. (Refer back to Figure 10.19)

Poly-lock nuts stick up higher than the valve covers. Then you can't put the valve covers on. The ignition coils are bolted to the valve covers, so you can't just throw them away. You could buy or make spacers but that would still allow oil leaks and you must take into consideration the cost.

If you have a lathe or favorite machine shop, you can shorten the ARP studs on the intake side, shorten the poly-locks, locate shorter lock screws, and try reassembling the valve train. If this doesn't fit under the valve covers, disassemble the studs and poly locks, remachine them, and try again. This is used in offshore racing where they want ultimate durability. Yes, this is a lot of work, but it does the job when durability is one of your main considerations.

The next way, and our way, is to use the Raylar rocker arm kit that uses the stock rocker studs and pushrods. It has a machined nut that bottoms out on the stock rocker stud. This saves you from the additional cost of buying special studs. In the kit you'll find special nuts that locate the rocker arms in the correct location to work with the non-adjustable valve train and stock pushrods. The stainless rockers are narrow (in width) and they don't interfere with any part of the head, nor do they need to be trimmed like some aluminum roller rockers. For further information on the non-adjustable valve train, go online and search for the following: "roller rocker valve train adjustment Gen7 BBC Vortec 8.1L."

Rocker Arm Adjusting Process

The first thing to do when adjusting the rocker arms is to oil the pushrods and install them in the correct locations.

Figure 10.22 In this photo you can see two pushrods going through their guide plates. This is the correct placement for the pushrods.

Figure 10.23 Here the rocker arms are set on the rocker studs with pushrods to check fitment.

Short pushrods are for the intake and long pushrods match with the exhaust. Be sure they seat positively in the hydraulic valve lifter and protrude through the pushrod guide plate at the top of the head (Figure 10.22). Now the fun begins. Larry has selected the stainless-steel rocker arms for the engine he's building. Remember, these come with their own special nuts and fit in the machined side of the trunnion. Place a rocker arm on top of each rocker arm stud with the flat side of the trunnion facing up (Figure 10.23). Be sure the roller tip of the rocker arm is sitting on the valve—not the pushrod! Using a ¼" nut driver, or a ¼" ratchet (with either a snap-on ¼" drive with a 7⁄16" thin wall socket or a ¼" drive with a 7⁄16" standard socket you ground down to fit) (Figure 10.24). Get ready to adjust the rockers.

Figure 10.24 The snap-on socket on the left is a thin-wall 7⁄16" socket. The socket on the right is a standard wall 7⁄16" socket ground down for clearance.

First, though, you must determine which lifters are on the cam lobes or on the cam base circle. If the lifter is on the lobe, it will be high relative to the dog bones. If it is on the base circle the lifter will be about even with the dog bone. You're going to start with the ones on the base circle, then rotate the crank 360 degrees and tighten the remaining rockers. Of the eight rockers, generally five will be on the base circle and three on the lobe. If there is a problem, it will be apparent quickly.

Next, find where the pushrod reaches "zero (0) clearance." With your nut driver on the nut inside the rocker, reach down and grab the pushrod. Lift it up and down while tightening the nut. When the pushrod can no longer move up and down—*STOP!* Now, loosen the nut just a bit and try to spin the pushrod back and forth as you slowly tighten the nut. When rotating the pushrod, the instant it stops you've reached zero clearance. Next you'll need to see how far the lifter plunger is compressed, and this is done using your ¼" ratchet.

With the handle pointing straight down, slowly tighten the nut. You'll be looking to make somewhere between

Figure 10.25 Larry has marked the number of turns with his socket that will bring the pushrod into adjustment.

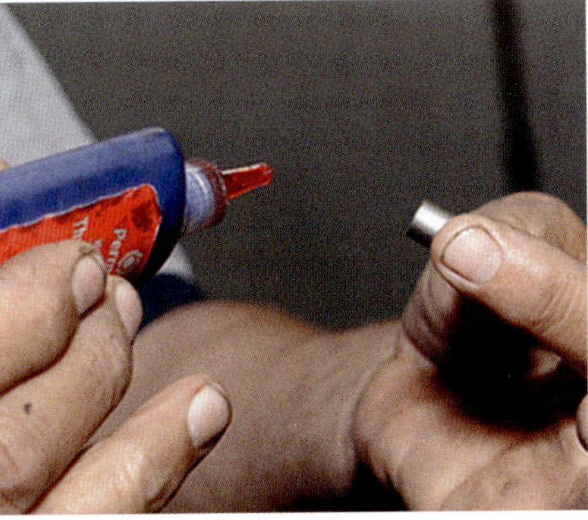

Figure 10.26 After tightening all the nuts, remove each one individually and put a drop of Loctite on the first three threads—then re-apply, finger tight.

one and two turns. Suppose you make 1-⅜-turns. It needn't be perfect. We judge by approximating ⅛-turn—for instance: one turn, one-⅛th turns, one-¼ turns—you get the idea. Use a paint marker or Sharpie to write that number on the intake side of the head, over the pushrod (Figure 10.25). When you've done all the rockers that were on the base circle, turn the crankshaft 360 degrees and do the remaining rockers and pushrods the same way. The reason for writing down the adjustment numbers is to be able to look at all the adjustments and compare them to one another.

Some of this is probably going to go south for you. Suppose you get 2-½ turns with your ¼" driver, or one that is out of range as compared to the other seven. Here are a few of the things that could be wrong:

- there could be air in the lifter
- the block may have returned from the machine shop with incorrect machining
- there could be a bad rocker
- the machine shop could have left the valve stems too long from the valve job, or likewise with the head.

Any of these could be the problem. Uncle Bob probably wouldn't care, but this is to be a high-performance engine and we want a lot more out of it.

If you think the problem lies in any of the above issues, start by switching parts from a good rocker train to the bad, and see if the problem follows. If it does follow, you know what parts you moved. If it didn't, you also know what you didn't move. When you're certain you know which part is out of range, adjust or replace it. Usually the repair is rather simple. If all of your numbers are out of range, more than two turns, you can put a shim under the rocker stud and raise them up. To remove one turn will require a shim of .040" thick under the stud. And if the turns are less than one, a longer pushrod will correct this. (.040" longer will change it by one turn) Usually a .060 longer pushrod will get you back in range. The reason for writing the turn's numbers on the intake surface is to be able to visually compare all the adjustments of the studs. If any of the adjustments are off, it will be apparent when you're done.

We've got one more thing to do. After you've tightened all the nuts hand tight and the adjustments look correct, remove each one of the nuts and put two drops of Loctite on the first three threads, now re-apply each nut to finger tight (Figure 10.26). You must go through the same process having the hydraulic lifter on the base circle. Go through and torque the nuts to 110 in-lbs. Then rotate the crankshaft 360 degrees and tighten the remaining nuts. It's a long project but you'll thank us in the long run.

Oil Pump

Let's flip the engine over and complete the things we need to do on the bottom side (Figure 10.27). The first thing we'll do is install the oil pump. If the engine were installed in the truck, the oil pump would be on the passenger side of the block. If you look closely at the engine in the illustration you can see where the pump sits and the hole for the oil pump intermediate shaft. This goes through to connect to the oil pump drive assembly. Larry inserts the shaft first, and then sets the pump on its main cap. Be sure the gears are synchronized before torquing your bolt (Figure 10.28). Torque the oil pump retainer bolt to 58–63 ft-lbs. It is always a good idea to confirm the clearances of the oil pump pick up to oil pan. No closer than ⅜" and no wider than ⅝".

Windage Tray

On the GM block, install the factory crankshaft windage tray. For the 4.500 stroke cranks, there is very little or no interference at all. With a 4.750 stroke crank, use 2-7⁄16" ARP head bolt washers on each leg stud to raise the tray away from the crank. You will also need to use a large screwdriver to move the tray away from the rod bolts as the

Figure 10.27 Ready for work on the bottom side. In the left-center of the picture is the oil pump boss. Just above that is the hole for the oil pump intermediate shaft.

Figure 10.30 These are the ⅛" spacers for checking the fit of the intake manifold.

Figure 10.28 Here is the oil pump installed. Look closely and you can see the intermediate shaft going from the pump down into the rear main cap.

crank turns. Finish the underside by installing the oil pan. Again, be sure you have a new gasket. The gasket is of the O-ring type and pushes into the groove in the oil pan. Put a blob of silicone in each of the four corners to seal these. Torque the bolts to 18 ft-lbs. (Figure 10.29). This intersection of the oil pan, the block, and the main caps, have the highest probability of an oil leak at the pan.

Installing the Intake Manifold

The first thing Larry does is to confirm the angles at the intake surfaces and the vertical gap clearances at the China rail. This is done with a pair of ⅛" thick aluminum plates cut and drilled to resemble the 8.1L gaskets (Figure 10.30). This is because the plates are the same thickness as the 8.1L intake gaskets compressed. With these plates set on the intake surfaces and your manifold set on top, it becomes immediately apparent if the angles of the intake surfaces and height of the China rail are correct. If the deck or head is milled at an incorrect angle, this will also show up on the intake surface angle and cause the engine to suck oil. If these angles look good, test fit the GM intake gaskets (silver steel-center with black O-rings), without the silicone sealant. Be sure you get the tangs on the bottom of the intake gasket to fit into the slots extending from the head gaskets (Figure 10.31). Remember these slots need to be bent down so as not to interfere with the bottom of the intake manifold.

Set the manifold on and check the bolt hole locations for bolt length. Silver bolts are 58 mm long and black bolts are 60 mm long. The black bolts are recommended replacements from GM. Move the manifold back and forth and watch for the bolts to drop into the holes in the heads. If they don't, find out why. There have been instances where the intake manifold bolt holes have been opened up to 5⁄16" or ⅜" to compensate for machined stacking

Figure 10.29 We've got the pan on now. Did you remember to put a blob of silicone into all four corners to seal the pan?

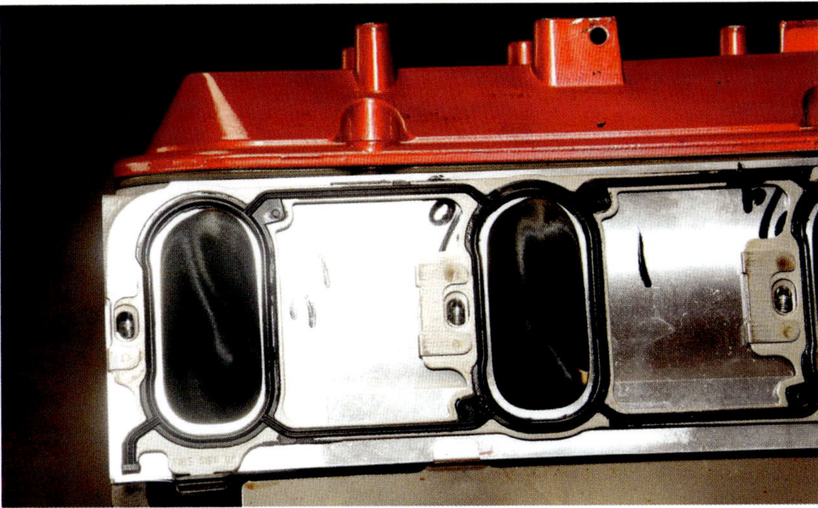

Figure 10.31 The intake manifold gasket has been installed. Down in the left-hand corner you can see the tab ("THIS SIDE UP") that fits into the tab of the head gasket. Be sure these are inserted.

Figure 10.32 Spread a giant bead of silicone on the front and rear China rails. This should fill in the gap when the intake manifold has been seated.

Figure 10.33 The intake manifold has been set into the valley.

tolerances. If this looks good, remove the manifold and set aside. Go look for your tube of gray or black silicone sealer and squeeze a big bead of sealer across the front and rear China rails. Better too much than not enough. You don't want a leak (Figure 10.32). Almost always, the supplied rubber seals will not compress correctly, so it's honorably deposited in the trash. Now is the time to set the manifold back on the engine, being careful not to wipe the silicone off the rails.

With the manifold on, drop the bolts back in their holes, move the manifold back and forth and watch for the bolts to drop into their holes again. Using a ¼" drive and a 10 mm socket, start in the middle and tighten the bolts down to almost contacting. Then go on to the rest in a circular pattern. When they are all started and almost contacting, go back to the middle and begin again. As you tighten all the bolts, you'll find the middle ones loose again. Then, when you finish the middle, you'll find the ends loose. So, repeat this process several times until they stay tight at 110 in-lbs. (Figure 10.33). When the manifold is tight, there should be silicone squeezing out between the manifold and block (Figure 10.34).

Accessory Drives

Things begin to pick up. Larry is installing the accessory drives now. The old engine was very sound, and all the parts were good, so we'll start by installing the water pump (Figure 10.35). Don't forget the gasket or you'll lose all your water on the first run! Four bolts hold it in place and must be torqued to 37 ft-lbs. The second of these parts is the water crossover pipe and its gaskets. Two bolts hold each side to the head. Remember earlier when we told you the freeze plugs went into the *rear* hole in the aluminum head? This is why (Figure 10.36). Now, torque each bolt to 37 ft-lbs. A third piece makes up the complete water system—the black hose you see in the illustration (Figure 10.37) connecting the crossover to the water pump. This is held with

Figure 10.34 Notice after the manifold bolts have been tightened that it has squeezed the silicone all the way across the China rail. Take a look at the rear rail and be sure you see the same thing.

Figure 10.35 Four bolts hold the water pump to the block and should be torqued to 37 ft-lbs.

Figure 10.36 The crossover pipe connects the two heads together—and does so where you may have incorrectly placed two freeze plugs. Don't forget the gaskets and torque the four bolts to 37 ft-lbs.

tension rings that can be applied with a pair of pliers.

There are two types of dampers in common use today. First, the standard GM 2500 and 3500 truck, 8" damper, that has both a four-groove and a six-groove pulley. Then, Mercury Marine and several other marine suppliers use a 5-½", six-groove pulley with a large 8" damper ring. There are, however, several more industrial and truck dampers in use. From GM, these dampers have no keyway as the engine is internally neutral balanced. It makes no difference where the damper is indexed.

To press on the damper for a normal rebuild, use the correct damper installer for the stock 8.1L crank (tool #J44900 or 16 × 1.50 metric thread). With the aftermarket steel cranks, the standard 454–502 crankshaft uses a ½ × 20 damper installer and works fine. In the supercharger or aftermarket steel crank world, the dampers need to be keyed to the steel crankshaft that comes with a 3⁄16" keyway machined in (Figures 10.38 and 10.39). This keeps the damper from spinning and coming off.

Use an anti-seize liquid or oil to keep the damper from galling on the crank. When pressed all the way on, put a ring of silicone around the washer that goes under the retainer bolt to keep oil from wicking out of the keyway. Tighten to 105 ft-lbs for the ½" bolt and 150 ft-lbs for the 16 mm.

Mount the power steering and accessory drive bracket with four bolts to the block, the alternator on top, and torque the bolts to 37 ft-lbs. Then add the alternator idlers and tensioners, torquing these to 37 ft-lbs. (Figure 10.40).

When using the aftermarket blocks, other than GM, the fuel pump boss interferes with the A/C bracket. To correct the issue, grind down the reinforcement on the back of the A/C bracket as shown, and it will fit perfectly (Figure 10.41).

Everyone is going to use a different carburetion system in their application. Rather than extend this chapter, we're going to include all of that information in the next chapter.

Figure 10.37 In this photo we've completed the front water package by connecting the crossover pipe to the water pump. That's the black rubber "L" shaped piece you see in the center. The clamps were put on with a regular pair of pliers.

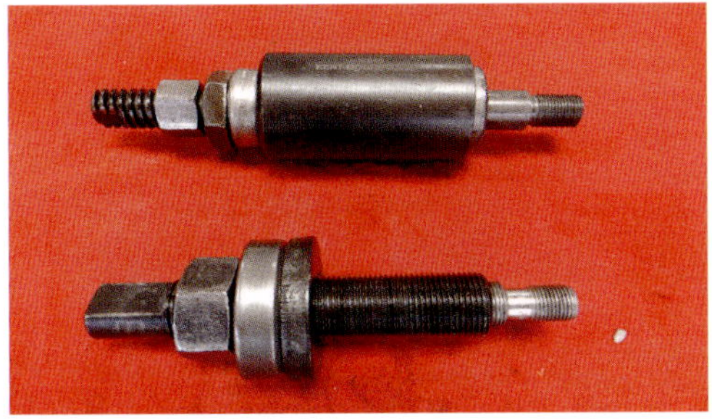

Figure 10.38 One of these tools will be required for damper installation.

Figure 10.39 As our engine is to be supercharged, Larry has selected a crank and damper with a 3/16" keyway. You can see this in the center of the damper at the top of the shaft.

Figure 10.40 This is our basic, finished engine. Everything's in place and Larry decided to put the belt(s) on to give it some "presence."

Figure 10.41 This is the A/C bracket with the reinforcement ground off the back.

Extra Tips

Silicone is a hidden danger. When you place the timing cover over the timing gears, we've seen occasions where the silicone has unintentionally been pushed into one of the bottom bolt holes. When this happened, the mechanic began to tighten the bolt down to torque specifications. As he screwed the bolt in, the bolt head never contacted the cover, so he just continued to tighten it until he broke the bolt! The moral is: be sure your bolt holes are clear all the way to the bottom and don't forget to torque the bolts.

Stroker Cranks

The 496 8.1 crankshaft was originally planned to be forged steel. The 1996 prototype 496 that I have has a 4.375 stroke steel crank made by Callies. Next was the production steel crank shaft made by Kellogg steel foundries in Michigan. This crankshaft has a distinct purple color tone to it and makes it easy to identify. These were used in the very early production engines and then a scattering of the 425 hp marine engines. The last group of stock steel 496 cranks ran out in 2010. Somewhere in the early 2001–2002's the GM bean counters got in the mix and decided it was cheaper to have a cast iron crank developed. This crank was used in all production truck engines from 2002 to current. This cast crank has a lot of extra material added to the rod journal cheeks to make it survive. It works fine up to 500–550 hp. All production crankshafts have a 4.375 stroke.

Figure 11.01 4.750 stroke crank installed in a GM 8.1 block making a 540 CID.

Figure 11.03 Shows a neutral balance flywheel needed for the internally balanced crankshaft.

Fitting Aftermarket Steel Stroker Cranks

The block pan rails of the 496 8.1L were designed wider than Gen 4, 5, or 6 blocks by about 1 inch and therefore have no interference problems with the 4.500 or the 4.750 stroke crankshaft.

With the traditional Gen 4, 5, or 6, there is generally grinding necessary to fit a 4.375 or bigger crank in between the oil pan rails of the block. It is also necessary to use a connecting rod designed for a stroker crank with cap screw rod bolts holding the cap together. This is to allow more clearance between the big end of the rod and the pan rails and cylinder sleeves. If not, the

Figure 11.02 The piston side of a PSI block with a 4.750 stroke crank in it.

rod bolts will hit the pan rail and bottom of the cylinders. With the correct rods, the 4.500 just drops in. The 4.750 stroke crank will also clear the pan rails without grinding but will need to have clearance ground between the rods and the bottom of the cylinder sleeves. The 4.500 crank is currently available, but the 4.750 stroke crank was made as a custom crank for a line of industrial engines and they have all been used to the best of my knowledge. One could be custom made but would be a very expensive, being a custom crank. The advantage of the 4.750 stroke was the huge torque they produced under 5000 rpm, and they worked very well in air boats and trucks.

Pistons

The only consideration for a custom stroker piston is to have clearance for the crankshaft counterweights at the bottom and the correct wrist pin location so the piston doesn't protrude above the block deck. This is because the added stroke not only pushes the piston up higher, it also pulls the piston down farther. If the pistons are not designed correctly, the piston and counterweights will collide at the bottom of the stroke or the top of the piston will hit the cylinder head and damage the pistons and rods. Custom stroker pistons are generally of the forged piston variety.

Figure 11.04 Cam being installed.

Figure 11.05 Block shown with cam, lifters, retainers, and spring retainer installed.

Figure 11.06 When installing the timing gear bolts, always use Loctite.

Figure 11.07 Completed 2004 and up truck timing gear set.

Figure 11.08 Make sure that the oil pump drive sits down completely on this boss before tightening the bolt. If not, it will break the ear. Use Loctite.

Figure 11.09 This photo shows the complete pistons, rings, and rods used with a forged, rotating assembly, 4.500 or 4.750 stroker kit.

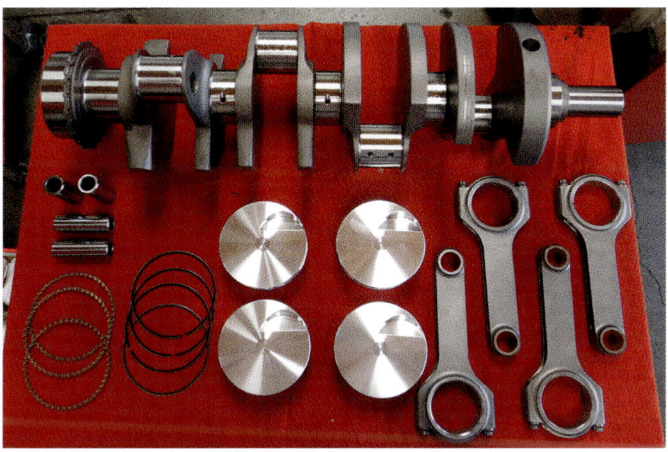

Figure 11.10 Here is the complete stroker kit. The crank, H-beam rods, forged pistons, and rings. Note how trim the forged steel rod journal throws are compared to the cast iron crank.

Figure 11.11 This photo shows the machining required for the long stroke 4.750 crank to clear the bottoms of the cylinder sleeves. The 4.500 stroke crank doesn't need this machining to clear the sleeves. It just drops in.

Figure 11.12 This is what happens when you put a supercharger on a stock 496 CID 8.1L marine engine with cast pistons.

Figure 11.13 Bent rods and shattered pistons.

12

Extra Tips, Tricks, and Notes

When Don and I set out to write this book I thought about the many ways to end this thing so that the reader would feel they had gained insider knowledge. I spend about half my time on the telephone answering the same questions over and over, so one afternoon I decided to start writing down the questions I was getting on the phone. It became clear to me that almost all of the questions people asked could be divided into about ten groups. So, to that end, I have squeezed them all into standard replies. Therefore, for your curiosity and edification, I give you "Larry's Top Ten Questions and Answers." I hope they solve many of the questions you have about the 496 CID 8.1L engines.

Iron Head Valve Springs

Many of the questions were about the iron head valve springs. Here's what I tell customers. The stock 8.1L spring is a basic beehive-designed spring with 90 lbs seat pressure that works very well in stock and mild performance engines with up to 0.500" lift and around 220–224 duration. If you replace the springs, go to around 110 lbs seat pressure. For the marine world you need a double valve spring. This is due to the durability issue. If one of the two springs break, the other spring keeps the valve from falling into the cylinder. I recommend a spring package of about 140 lbs seat pressure. For all the spring suppliers that don't know, the 8.1L uses a standard Gen 4, 5, or 6 valve spring with a ⅜" retainer and locks in at the standard installed spring height.

Head Bolts for the Iron Head

GM recommends that the stock 8.1L head bolts be thrown in the trash and new ones purchased after using them once. This appears questionable. Early on, when there weren't any ARP head studs, I used the stock head bolts over two or three times on dyno thrashes. Seldom did the head bolts stretch (yes, some did, but not many). What I would do is clean the threads with a wire brush, then lay out the bolts with the threads interlocking. This way you can see if any of the threads stretched. I found mostly good results. For the iron heads, the bolts torque to 65 lbs for the long ones and 60 lbs for the shorter ones. ARP doesn't make 10-mm bolts long enough for the iron heads, although they do make a stud kit. My aluminum heads have the head bolt bosses at a different height to work with my ARP head bolt kit.

Engine Mounts

The stock 8.1L motor mount on the driver's side tends to pull apart frequently. This is due to the high torque of the engine. There is a simple fix for this. When you get your new motor mount, drill a ⅜" hole through the middle of the mount and put a ⅜" × 3" long bolt through the hole. Use a nyloc nut to secure the bolt but don't tighten the bolt too tightly. This way the mount can still isolate the vibrations, but as the engine tries to pull the mount apart, the bolt will prevent this from happening. This will work on both sides.

8.1L Engines and Newer Trucks

Let's talk about how to put 8.1L engines in a 2010 or newer truck (or car) with a six- or eight- speed automatic LS transmission. GM makes a transmission adapter kit (part number 19154766) for the small block that almost works. It has a ⅜" thick spacer that gives room for the stock torque converter and the bolts necessary to attach the transmission. Everything else in the kit goes in the trash. One side effect of this kit is that it either moves the transmission back or the engine forward and the stock mounts will need some adjusting. Also, you get to make a flex plate to fit as there are no stock flex plates that have the correct crank flange or torque converter bolt pattern. The easiest answer is to use the 8.1 flex plate and modify the torque converter mounting holes. The computer wiring from the LS is compatible to the 8.1L and takes just a few modifications to get it running. The 8.1L must be fitted with an X58 count crank reluctor and an X4 cam gear.

8.1L Accessory Drives

The stock truck and marine accessory drives work very well for their intended purpose. However, if you are building something cool, you don't want all that iron on the front of the engine. The way to get past this is to look at a

1968–1975 big-block Corvette belt drive or an aftermarket serpentine belt drive. These components come in aluminum and fit the Gen 5 and 6 engines. Ask for a tall-deck mounting bracket configuration. There are some dimensions that are not exactly the same, and the bolt holes will be for SAE fasteners, but it can be made to work. It would use either a short or long water pump and a corresponding neutral balance dampener from a Gen 4, 5 or 6 big block.

Computer Tuning

Trucks

For trucks, if you call a computer tuning company and ask them if they can tune your 2001–2006 truck computer, they will probably say no. If you ask the same person if they can tune a 1997–2004 Corvette, they will probably say sure, when can you bring it in? The point here is that the computer in your 8.1L truck is exactly the same as the Corvette computer. The person that you spoke with is absolutely capable of tuning your truck computer, they just don't know it yet. They have no interest in learning about a truck computer, and don't know they are the same unless you explain it to them. If you take the time to explain it, there are many people who would love to take your money and tune your truck computer.

Marine

Mercury uses the Motorola 555 computer and limits licensed tuning companies to very few. Whipple Superchargers is the most well-known, Mark at Precision Marine in New Orleans is another, and Alexi at Boostpower is a third. There may be others, but I haven't used them. The MEFI is the second most popular marine computer and you can find programming software on the internet. From there, Volvo, Crusader, Marine Power, Pleasurecraft and others all use variations of their own proprietary computers and need to be consulted about custom programming.

Engine Oil

Nowadays, there is no reason to not run on synthetic engine oil. There is not a bad synthetic oil made. There are only a few manufactures of oil and only the additive package changes. If you choose multi-viscosity oil in the 10–40 range and change the oil on a 3000–4000-mile schedule, there is nothing better you can do for your engine.

Spark Plugs

I get lots of calls about what type of spark plug to use and what the heat range should be. There are no magic spark plugs and they all do the same thing—initiate the combustion process. Engineers have worked out an application for the stock plug and heat range. If there were free horsepower to be made with a different spark plug, they would have done so. If you are running your engine harder than designed, with more compression, or a supercharger, then a colder range spark plug will keep from burning the porcelain up or starting preignition. The stock plug gap of .060" works fine with the coil-on-plug ignition system and naturally aspirated. For a supercharged engine, a gap of .045" is better. I would not go more than two heat ranges colder.

Headers and Exhaust Systems

Once again, we are not telling you how to build a performance exhaust. There are many books that deal with HOW to build a performance exhaust in depth.

Trucks and Cars

In general, the stock truck exhaust manifolds work well for low-performance engines, however it is like blowing through a straw. Yes, it works, but leaves a lot to be desired. Also, there is no reason to *want* back pressure in your exhaust system. In the automotive world it is used to make the EGR system work. Never in the racing world would you see anybody putting some item on their exhaust to restrict and cause back pressure, unless it is a turbocharger or muffler to limit sound. In the real world, there is usually a level of sound that is mandated to keep from pissing off other people, or groups of people, who don't get the same enjoyment from your open exhaust. This is why we must work with mufflers and some form of exhaust on our vehicles, and this creates two categories that need to be dealt with.

Exhaust Pulses

First let's discuss the exhaust pulses that leave the head. In normal engines you have an exhaust manifold that simply connects the ports of the head to the exhaust pipe to remove the exhaust gasses. There is no thought as to how best to do this, just packaging which is good enough, and works fine in a nonperformance truck or car. In the performance world, it is better to have each exhaust port with its own separate pipe to reap the benefits of scavenging. This is the concept of the prior exhaust pulses pulling out the present exhaust pulse of gas. This scavenging improves the combustion chamber filling efficiency. In general, a set of long tube headers is the most efficient for scavenging, and more efficient than a set of shorty headers. Shorty headers are a compromise that is better than a stock exhaust manifold and will connect to the stock head pipe for smog certifications. Most everyone has some understanding of this process and I won't go any deeper into it. What I will say is that there are general rules to use. In a nutshell, if you are looking for low-rpm torque, you want a smaller diameter header pipe. For the 8.1L, start with a 1-⅞" diameter tube and get it as long as you can to the collector. If you want your hp at a higher rpm, you will want a larger header tube such as 2" or 2-⅛" diameters with a shorter length to the collector. Banks motor home headers, I have heard, use small pipes (1-¾") in diameter and almost four feet long to the collector. This is because a motor home's engine requires low rpm torque. For a person running the engine hard at 6000 rpm, they would be more interested in 2-⅛" diameter pipes and 32" long tubes to the collector. Packaging with headers is usually a secondary concern. Another concern is to never use a set of headers with a header flange less than ⅜" thick. Banks uses ½" flanges. If you don't, you will forever be chasing exhaust-flange leaks. Use 3" diameter exhaust pipes minimum to the mufflers. Fortunately, the 8.1 truck came standard with 3" pipes. The stock catalytic converters are 3" in diameter and have almost no restriction to exhaust flow. If they are not plugged, you might as well keep them on.

Mufflers

Second is the muffler. The stock 8.1L came with mufflers that have dual 3" pipes in and dual 2-¾" outlets. In GM's infinite wisdom they closed down the dual outlets to one 2-¾" pipe and went all the way out the back. If you add the second 2-¾" outlet pipe, it makes a pretty good, quiet exhaust. From here your favorite muffler shop is your best friend. There are many low-back pressure mufflers with 3" tailpipes to be had. As always, a lower back pressure exhaust system comes with a louder exhaust sound.

Marine Applications

The majority of 496 engines were supplied to Mercury to marinize. Of course there are many other engine suppliers who also used this engine package. For the 375 and 425 hp packages, Mercury designed an exhaust manifold that actually had good air flow and would flow 525 hp of air up into the risers. All you need to do is lift off the riser, remove the turbrolator plate, make a Frisbee out of it and reassemble. Now you're good to go. From here, the next steps are determined by the specific boat manufacturer. There are really good and really poor exhaust tailpipe routings depending on where the engine is placed relative to the transom exhaust outlets. Some tailpipes go straight out the back, which is good. Others take a winding Z-shape trip from the risers to the transom, which creates a lot of restrictions, which is bad. If the Captain's Call exhaust system is installed, the valves and routing also make a restriction to the exhaust. Again, it is the complete exhaust system, all the way to the transom, that is important. The majority of 496 engine suppliers use the standard 454–502 cast iron exhaust manifolds with square internal porting that restrict air flow and simply hook up the exhaust. There is no attention to performance air flow. There are many aftermarket suppliers of marine cast aluminum performance manifolds and all of these are an improvement over stock. However, my hands down favorite is the dual wall stainless steel tube header made by CMI. They are quite expensive because of all the work in making them, but they have the best engineering and performance gains. Used with a well-engineered tailpipe and dry cooling system, there is almost no back pressure and the scavenging is as good as it gets in a marine environment.

Appendix

Raylar 525 hp Kit Installation Instructions

RAYLAR

525 hp 496 CID

496 8.1L Engines Mercury, Indmar, Crusader, Volvo

2001–2004 cool fuel 1 mag or HO engines

2005–2010 cool fuel 2 mag or HO engines

Certified mechanic or qualified marine technician

Please read and familiarize yourself with these instructions before beginning any work on the 496 8.1L engine.

Note: Before starting the installation, check the Raylar kit for damaged or missing parts. Verify that all components on the parts list are ready for installation.

- The Raylar kits are best installed with the engine removed from the boat.
- All cooling systems on the motor must be drained before removing parts and installing Raylar parts.
- It is recommended that the engine have a compression test done on all eight cylinders. On stock 496 the cold cranking compression should be approximately 155–165 psi.
- If any cylinders are low more than 10 psi, a leak down test should be done to ascertain leak-down percentages as well as isolate whether the leakage is from valves or from piston and ring areas. If the losses are from the valves the Raylar heads will solve that problem.
- However, if the loss in psi is because of piston, cylinder, or rings, these need to be corrected before the Raylar kit is installed. If not corrected, serious engine damage can occur, which Raylar will not be responsible for.

Removal

1. **Computer and Wiring Removal (Remove/Disconnect the following)**

- Look for the six connectors
  - Cam sensor on front of cam cover
  - Single brown wire to temp sender on front water crossover
  - Low water pressure sensor on raw water pump (late-model 2005 and later have this psi sender on the rear heat exchanger)
  - The 3-wire connector to the throttle position sensor
  - Right exhaust manifold over heat sender
  - Left exhaust manifold over heat sender
- Mounting plate for the engine control module (ECM) and relays—two 10 mm nuts to the side of the fuel rail and two 13 mm nuts to the exhaust manifold.
- Under the computer, the two 10-pin connectors. One for the coil packs and one for the fuel injectors.
- On the other side, the 10-pin connector for the other coil pack.
- Check for the power wiring for the fuel pump or pumps. Roll back the loom to the rear of the engine.
- MAP sensor connector, intake air-temperature (IAT) sensor connector, and the idle air control (IAC) connector on the manifold.
- On the lower left- and right-hand sides of the block, two white connectors for the knock sensor.
- Just above the oil filter pad are the oil temp and oil pressure senders.
- On the rear bell housing studs will be one or two black ground wires.

- Remove the rear engine lifting plate as it will have the Merc 10-pin connector and the Merc Cathode box on it (on the later loom, Merc puts a twist lock 14-pin connector on top of the engine)
- Next will be the yellow starter wire and the red battery power wire. Also, in the lower front, will be the 2-wire alternator connector, the red battery charge terminal, and the black ground wires. Be careful when removing these two 10 mm nuts so as not to twist off the wire ends.
- Remove the loom and set it aside.

2. **Exhaust Removal**

- Remove the 1" water cooling hoses on the lower check valves, right and left side.
- Remove the oil filter support bracket, being careful not to kink the hoses.
- Each manifold has a water temp overheat sensor. Make sure these are unplugged as the sensors are fragile. Each manifold has four long and four short 8 mm stainless bolts, which require a 13-mm socket. *Note: This is generally a two-person job. The early manifold castings are aluminum; cumbersome but not too heavy. The late manifolds are cast iron and are very heavy. You will need two people to remove them.*
- Remove the six middle bolts, loosen the two remaining bolts, have someone support the weight, and remove the last two bolts.
- Get out of the way, remove the manifolds, and set aside.

3. **Intake Manifold Removal**

- At the rear of the manifold you will find the ⅜" fuel feed line. You will need a fuel line connector removal tool to remove it. Watch out for spraying fuel. There are ten #6 bolts, five on each side, that need to be removed. Set the manifold aside.
- On early fuel rails, there will be a ⅜" fuel feed, a 5⁄16" fuel return and an adjustable pressure regulator that will be used later to adjust fuel psi. See if the regulator can be adjusted. If not, a new GM regulator will be needed. (It uses a #10 anti-tamper Torx bit which can be purchased at most auto parts stores.)
- The later fuel rails only have a ⅜" fuel feed and will need a Raylar adjustable pressure regulator at the fuel pump.

2007–2010 Bolt GM black	GM #11609264
2001–2005 Regulator fuel rail	GM #12574986
2005–2010 Regulator Raylar	BP REGULATOR
2001–2010 Grommet Cover	GM #12557831

- Remove the valley tray and set aside. Remove the oil pump drive and lifter bar retainer and set aside. Check and see if you have black or silver manifold bolts. You will need black bolts because they are longer.

4. **Valve Cover Removal**

- Inspect the rubber grommets under the bolts. Sometimes they tear and will leak. Keep the valve cover O-ring in its groove so it keeps its shape.
- Remove the rocker arms and set aside.
- Remove the pushrods and set aside. The pushrods will be reused, the rockers will not.

5. **Cooling System Removal**

- If not done already, drain the coolant in the block.
- The best way is to remove the two 18 mm block plugs directly above the pan rail.
- Remove the U-shaped hose from the water pump to the coolant crossover as this contains coolant also. Don't make a mess; use a container to save the coolant as it can be reused.
- Remove the heat exchanger, the hoses on the end, and the two big clamps in the center.
- Remove the support from the raw water pump support studs to the coolant crossover. It will have either a tensioner or an idler pulley. Between the crossover and water pump is a hose clamp that uses a ¼" nut driver to remove. Loosen this. Pay attention to its location as it must be reassembled the same way.
- Next, use a ⅜" drive, 15 mm wobble socket, and extension to remove the four crossover retaining bolts to the head. The dip stick is held to the crossover with a 6-mm bolt. Remove this and the dip stick will just float. Don't try to remove it. Pull the crossover forward and up to work it off the water pump.
- Get the two gaskets off the front of the heads and inspect their condition.
- Next, four 15 mm bolts for the water pump and off it comes, two more gaskets, and inspect. *Note: Now is a very good time to remove the end caps on the heat exchanger to make sure it is clean.*

6. **Damper Removal**

- Remove the three Allen screws holding the 6-groove pulley to the damper, set aside.
- Remove the damper retainer bolt. For references, scribe a line across the damper and the end of the crank. This engine is neutrally balanced, but just in case. Using a standard 3-bolt puller and three 10 mm 496 head bolts.
- Remove the damper and set aside.

7. **Timing Cover Removal**

- Remove the six 10 mm bolts holding the timing cover.
- Gently pull the cover off from the top, paying attention to the two dowel pins down low on the front of the block.

8. **Remove Cylinder Heads, Careful!!! They are 76 lbs each.**

- There are eighteen bolts in total: twelve long, two medium, and four short.
- Remove both cylinder heads from the engine. Carefully inspect all the tops of the pistons for cracks from the eyebrow to the ring land. On cast pistons cracks will show up here first.
- Also, inspect the cylinder walls for any unusual wear or damage. Pay attention to any cylinder scoring that may be greater in one cylinder than the others.
  - This could be an indication of problems in specific cylinders due to improper piston ring fit or overheating.
  - Address any problems and repairs before proceeding with the kit installation.
  - Some vertical marks and light scores marks are normal, but they should not be deep enough to feel with a fingernail when scraped across.
  - If all looks good, carefully clean the top of the block. Be careful not to scratch or gouge the deck surface as this may affect proper head gasket sealing.
  - Make sure all carbon and dirt is removed from all cylinders. Blow out the cylinders when done.
- Set the right and left head gaskets on the deck of the block and check to make sure the water passages in the *rear of the block* match the openings in the gasket.
  - If the gaskets are installed incorrectly the engine will overheat and serious damage may result!
  - Use a 10 mm/1.50 tap to *clean all the head bolt holes in the deck surface.* This is important!
  - Locate the fourteen 100 mm long bolts and four 60 mm short bolts for each head. The new ARP head bolts use a stainless flat washer between the bolt and the aluminum head. You must use GM thread sealer PN#1050026 or equivalent on the head bolt threads where they go into the block. The threads are exposed to the water in the block.
  - If you don't use sealer, THEY WILL LEAK COOLANT. Best to use too much than not enough in this situation!

Installation

1. **Cylinder Head Installation**

- Remove the Raylar heads from their packaging and inspect them. If all is well and gasket surfaces are clean and dry, set them carefully on the engine (36 lbs). The heads are interchangeable.
- Do not use any sealers, coatings, or gasket cements on the new Cometic MLS gaskets. They are designed for dry installation only!
- Install the head bolts with washers and plenty of sealant.
- Torque correctly in the center out, radial pattern. First to just snug, then all to 30 ft-lb torque, then all to 50 ft-lb torque. Then the 100 mm long bolts get torqued to 55 ft-lb.
- When you are done, go back over them at least once more to verify all are evenly torqued down.
- DO NOT OVER TORQUE THE BOLTS. It is not needed and will damage the block threads.

2. **Camshaft Swap**

- Turn the crankshaft so the timing mark on the crank gear and the mark on the cam gear line up.
- Remove the three cam gear retainer bolts and remove the gear and chain. Set aside.
- Remove the cam retainer, the lifter guides, and lifters. Set these in the valley.
- Remove the cam, being careful not to scratch the cam bearings. Check the new cam for any damage. If ok, liberally lube the cam lobes and journals.

- Slide the new cam in carefully. Replace the cam retainer and bolts. Put two drops of Loctite per bolt.
- Inspect the roller lifters for any roughness. If there is, replace the lifters!
- Oil and reinstall the roller lifters.
- Reinstall the lifter guides.
- Reinstall the guide retainer and its four bolts.
- Reinstall the oil pump drive. Make sure it drops in all the way.
- Loctite and torque the bolt.
- Next, use the cam gear to turn the cam so the alignment mark on the cam gear lines up with the crank mark. Using a straight edge helps here.
- Install the cam gear and chain. Check alignment again!
- Loctite and tighten bolts to 20 ft-lb.
- Remove the rubber gasket from the timing cover, clean the gasket and its grove, removing any old silicone sealer and reinstall the gasket.
- Clean the block and oil pan. Place a small blob of gray GM silicone sealer at the corner of the block and oil pan junction.
- Carefully push the timing cover back over and onto the dowels on the block with the bottom going in first.
- Once the cover is in place, reinstall the six bolts and tighten. Using a harmonic balancer installation tool, reinstall the balancer with its reference mark lined up on the crank snout.
- Reinstall the dampener retainer bolt and torque to specs.

3. **Now that the heads, cam and lifters are installed you can start putting in the pushrods, long exhaust, and short intake, making sure they seat in the lifter cup.**

- Take each roller rocker after oiling it, and install it on a rocker stud, making sure to have the TRUNNION SEAT UP.
- Install a new AFN rocker retainer nut onto each stud making sure that it threads down into the trunnion body of each rocker. Once again check to make sure that the trunnion is right side up.
- To tighten the rocker nuts, do not use any tool bigger than a ¼" drive socket set!
- With both valves closed and lifters on the cam base circle, starting at cylinder #1 TDC and going through the firing order, tighten the AFN nuts until the pushrod stops spinning in your fingers. This is 0 clearance between the lifter and valve.
- At this point it should take between one and two turns to seat the AFN nut. Don't over tighten these nuts. 120 in-lb MAX!
- When this is done, bar the engine over several complete revolutions to make sure there is no binding or valve contact.

4. **Reinstall the water pump, then the water crossover between the front of the heads.**

5. **Reinstall the tensioner, brackets, and belt.**

6. **Install the 1-⅜" freeze plugs with a small smear of sealer and tap them flush into the holes in the back of the heads. Don't forget to tighten the ¼" clamp between the crossover and pump.**

7. **Intake Manifold Installation**

- If all looks good, reinstall the valley cover plate being careful that all four locating tabs are down against the head intake surface and snapped in place.
- Bend down the four tabs of the Cometic head gaskets so they don't hold up the intake manifold.
- Place the intake gaskets on the heads' surfaces and lock them into the tabs of the head gaskets. Using GM gray silicone gasket sealer, lay a large bead of sealer on the clean top block rail at each end of the block. This bead should touch and cover the corners of the intake gaskets.
- Once this bead and gaskets are in place, carefully and evenly lower the Raylar intake manifold into place.
- Use a couple of the intake bolts (BLACK) to check alignment, while checking to see if the manifold is level right to left.
- USE ANTI-SIEZE on the intake manifold bolts and thread in by hand as much as possible to ensure the manifold is aligned and the bolts are not cross threaded.
- Check the gaskets to make sure they are not sliding down while the manifold is being tightened down.
- Tighten the bolts evenly from side to side; middle out, to ensure the manifold is pulled down evenly, 106 in-lb.
- The gasket cement should be squishing out. Let it dry and cut it off later if you want.

8. **Injector Removal**

- Take the previously removed stock intake manifold, fuel rail, and injector assembly and carefully remove the eight green injector retainer clips.
- Remove the connectors from all eight injectors.
- Remove the two wire clips from the crossover and discard.
- Disconnect the harness clips from the fuel rail and set the harness aside.
- Locate the steel retainer clip at the junction of each fuel rail with the crossover tube.
- With a die grinder and carbide cutter, CAREFULLY remove the outer edge of these retainers until they split apart to allow the fuel rail crossover to separate.
- DANGER, GAS WILL COME OUT, DANGER, GAS WILL COME OUT, DANGER!!
- Be careful, no sparks, smoking, fires, anything!!! Get all the fuel out of the FUEL RAIL.
- Remove the blue O-rings and save.
- Test fit the new Raylar fuel crossover to the new manifold and old fuel rails. Do not use the crossover O-rings for this test!
- Lube the O-rings on the bottom of the injectors and set the rails on the correct side of the manifold.
- The crossover will only fit one way. When the crossover fits in the fuel rails correctly, the O-ring shoulder stops go completely inside the fuel rails.
- Now push the injectors into their respective holes in the manifold.
- Check carefully as the injectors are being pushed into place that the O-rings do not bulge out, dislodge, get pinched, or cut while sliding into their holes.
- The rails and injectors should fit down tightly on the manifold and the crossover shoulder should stay completely inside the receiver.
- The retainer bolt holes should have a slight compression.
- If all is well, now take it apart, put the O-rings on the crossover and set it aside.

9. **Injectors Installation**

- The #2, 4, 6, and 8 injector connector wires need to be fished under the center of the Raylar manifold.
- A wire hook will be useful here. Make sure the correct cylinder connectors go to the correct side of the manifold.
- With that done, the fuel rails and crossover are reassembled with the O-rings and worked in.
- Watch the O-rings of the crossovers and injectors for fit.
- When it is installed correctly, use the 6 mm short bolts to secure it down. Look it over again. You don't want fuel leaks!
- The crossover should be very stable and not move.
- Now put the green locks back in the injector connecters and connect to their correct injectors.
- The connecters are numbered so make sure you put the correct connecter on the correct cylinder!
- This fit is critical to prevent any high-pressure fuel leaks. After installation of the engine but prior to starting and running the engine, the crossover and injector O-ring seals should be checked with fuel pressure and the pump on. The injector fit and seal can only be checked with the engine fuel pressure on. When first started, carefully check and inspect for leaks!
- When doing these fuel leak tests, it is a good time to bleed the air out of the fuel rails by way of the Schrader valve and fuel pressure gauge. The gauge will also be needed to set the fuel pressure to 51 lb. No vacuum. This is required because of the higher hp.
    - 2001–2004 Merc Engines
        - Remove the plastic cover from the existing cool fuel assembly on the lower left side of the engine by the left motor mount. There is an existing pressure regulator on top front of the fuel cooler.
        - Unthread the steel fuel line from the front of this regulator and reinstall the brass fuel line plug included in the kit.
        - Take the 5⁄16" black fuel hose supplied with the kit and attach this fuel hose to the steel line removed using the brass coupler included in the kit.
        - Tighten these fuel line fittings carefully to properly seal them and prevent fuel leaks.
        - Route this fuel hose back along the bottom left side of the block and up to the factory 5⁄16" fuel return connector on the fuel rail.

  - Using a push-on fitting fuel line removal tool, remove the existing return line cap from the fuel rail and plug the new 5⁄16" rubber hose, push on the fitting end onto this location.
  - The primary fuel feed hose can now be reattached to the fuel rail. The fuel pressure is now adjusted with the regulator on the fuel rail, pump running, engine off, and no vacuum. 51 psi.
  - You need a #10 anti-tamper Torx bit to turn the regulator adjusting screw. If the screw won't turn and strips out, you will need to remove the snap ring that holds in the regulator and get a replacement regulator.
- 2005–2010 Merc Engines
  - Fuel pressure regulator. It is located on top of the fuel pump on the right front of the engine. It is held in by two Allen screws.
  - Remove these and remove the regulator.
  - The replacement Raylar regulator is simply lubed and pushed back in the hole.
  - Reinstall the two Allen screws. Use the correct size Allen wrench to adjust the regulator screw and be sure to tighten the lock nut. You should also put a drop of paint on the threads.
  - The pressure is set at 51 psi. Pump running, engine off, with no vacuum.

10. Intake manifold

- From the original manifold, you will need to remove these parts:
  - Remove the three 10 mm nuts holding the throttle body and linkage, set it aside.
  - Remove the three 6 mm studs and screw them into the Raylar manifold, same place.
  - Next, the 10 mm bolt holding the MAP sensor. Take the sensor and its grommet and insert them into the back of the new manifold plenum.
  - Remove the intake air temperature (IAT) sensor and screw it in next to the manifold absolute pressure (MAP) sensor. Remove the idle air control (IAC) motor and spacer plate. Be careful with the gaskets as you still need them.
  - Install the base on the plenum with the two 10 mm bolts, hose nipple down. Then attach the IAC motor with the two Allen screws.
  - Unscrew the 10 mm bolt that holds down the oil fill tube from the manifold. Remove the tube from the manifold; it is very tight.
- To reinstall the tube in the Raylar manifold there are two common ways.
  - First way is to bend the mounting tab to line up with the bolt hole in the throttle body mount. This makes it very solid.
  - The second way we have seen people do it, is put a screw through the new manifold oil fill tube and into the steel oil fill tube from the original manifold to hold it in place and use either silicone or JB weld to permanently attach it to the manifold.

11. Throttle body

- Remove the 1⁄8" spacer plate and progressive linkage and save the hardware.
- Save one gasket and put it on the three studs already screwed into the Raylar manifold now.
- Increase the size of the hole in the throttle plate to 5⁄16" and install the throttle body with the three 10 mm nuts. This will allow enough air to pass through the throttle body to still idle and set the throttle position sensor (TPS) at 0.6 volts. The 375 hp has a 3⁄16" hole; the 425 hp has a 19⁄64" or just less than 5⁄16 ".
- For our starting point, we use 5⁄16". Idle rpm in a HO computer is 650 rpm. This is what you want it set at. Now route the 3⁄4" IAC hose under the plenum from the throttle body to the IAC block in the rear.
- For reference, the BP203 cam gets a 5⁄16" hole, and the BP206 cam gets 3⁄8" in the throttle body.
- The Raylar throttle arm lever is attached to the throttle body with a spacer and 1⁄4" screw that the original progressive linkage donates.
- Use the spacer and 1⁄4" bolt to attach the lever to the throttle body.

12. Wiring and Computer

- Now you can start piling all that lovely wiring and computer back on top of the engine.
- It is very self-explanatory where the wires and connectors go too, as they only connect to their specific connectors.
- Under the computer support plate it gets very tight. Be careful not to pinch or damage the wiring.
- Another good idea is to drill a hole through the computer mounting plate to allow adjusting the

fuel pressure regulator after the computer is mounted.

- For those who want to beautify their engines, we have a computer relocation plate that moves the computer to the rear of the head. It requires understanding of wiring and some minor wire extending, but it cleans up the appearance of the top and valve cover area.
- For those who are very competent in wiring Raylar also has a coil relocation kit. It takes the coils off the valve covers and puts them down under the exhaust headers. This requires somebody to be very comfortable with rewiring, but the results are worth it.

13. Invest in a Scanning/Diagnostic Tool

We recommend either a Merc scanner or Rinda Technologies DIACOM for Merc engines, and I can't say this enough times! My first question to a customer is always, "What did the scan tool say?" We cannot help if we don't know the diagnostics. If you don't want to buy one, find someone who has one: it will save you so much time in the long run. Considering the investment in your boat and engine it just makes dollars and sense. It isn't that big of an investment and you can rent it to your friends! You will need to check voltages and scan codes to dial in your engine. If you have any issues down the road or on the lake, a diagnostic tool can save your whole vacation.

Appendix

Torquing Specifications

Part	*Torque*	*Hardware*
Cam/crank sensor screw	106 in-lbs	#6 screw
Spark plugs	15 ft-lbs	
Coil	106 in-lbs	
Camshaft gear bolts	22 ft-lbs	#8 × 1.25-mm
Cam retainer plate	106 in-lbs	
Timing cover	106 in-lbs	
Windage tray nuts	37 ft-lbs	Nine nuts
Oil pump bolt	56 ft-lbs	
Oil pan bolts	18 ft-lbs	
Oil level sensor	15 ft-lbs	
Oil pump drive bolt	18 ft-lbs	
Main caps (inner)	110 ft-lbs	
Main caps (outer)	100 ft-lbs	
Lifter guide retainer	18 ft-lbs	Four bolts
Stock rocker arm nuts	26 ft-lbs	
Raylar roller rocker nut	110 in-lbs	Red Loctite
Rocker studs	47 ft-lbs	
Rocker covers	106 in-lbs	
Accessory bolts	37 ft-lbs	
Flywheel	74 ft-lbs	
Harmonic balancer (damper)	189 ft-lbs	16-mm bolt size
Harmonic balancer (damper)	steel crank	½" bolt
All with ½" SAE threads	85 ft-lbs	
Iron heads	65 ft-lbs on long bolts 60 ft-lbs on short bolts	
Aluminum heads	55 ft-lbs on Long bolts 50 ft-lbs on short bolts	
Intake manifold ¼" ratchet and 10 mm socket	110 in-lbs	

Appendix

Short Block Parts and Sizes

Quantity	*Item Name*	*Size/Description*	*Part Number*
	SHORT BLOCK		
1	Crank Washer	16 mm	23504011
1	Crank Bolt	16 mm	14022672
3	Timing Chain Cam Bolts		11515757
1	Timing Chain Gear, Single Row		
	2001*		
	2002–2003*		
	2004 + Up		
1	Timing Chain, Single Row		
1	Timing Chain-Crank Gear, Single Row		
1	Timing Chain Cover		
	2001-2003		12566113
	2004 + Up		12589846
	Timing Chain Cover to Block Seal		12556370
6	Timing Chain Cover Bolts	6 × 1.0 × 30 mm	11517591
1	Timing Chain Cover Seal, Crank		12580743
	Timing Chain Cover Seal, Pin Locater		12554553
1	Cam Position Sensor		
	2001 Black		12575182
	2002–2004 White	213–1064	12575183
	2005 + Up Long	213–3529	12585545
	O-ring		
1	#6 Bolt × 15 mm for Position Sensor		11516361
1	Cam Retainer Plate		10168501
2	Cam Retainer Screws #6 Torx		11515151
	Cam		
2	Block Drain Plugs		11609916
1	Oil Filter Adapter Fitting		3853870
2	Oil Pressure Relief Valves		
	Truck	11 psi	25013765
	Marine	30 psi	25161284
4	Deck Dowel Sleeves		12558081

Quantity	*Item Name*	*Size/Description*	*Part Number*
	GM Roller Lifter Kit		12371056
16	Hydraulic Roller Lifters		17120060
8	Dog Bone Retainers		12551397
1	Lifter Guide Retainer		12551399
4	Lifter Guide Retainer Bolt	8 × 20 mm	11515757
1	Oil Pump Drive		12568356
1	Oil Pump Drive Bolt		11515756
1	Crankshaft Sensor	213–1556	12575172
1	Crankshaft Sensor Bolt	6 × 15 mm	12562852
1	Oil Pump Mounting Bolt	10 × 60 mm × 1.5	12557507
1	Oil Pump, High Volume		10778C Melling
1	Oil Pump Pick Up (motor home and marine)		
1	Windage Tray		12590688
	Windage Tray Main Studs		12559668
9	Windage Tray Retainer Nuts		11516077
12	Oil Pan Bolts	8 × 30 mm	11515758
1	Oil Pan with Tray Bolts		
1	Oil Pan Gasket		12567777
1	Oil Pan Separator Tray		
12	Oil Pan Separator Tray Bolts	6 × 15 mm	
1	Crankshaft	Cast	89017574
6	Crankshaft to Flywheel Bolt	11 × 25 mm	11609297
1	Dampener, Stock		
2	Oil Pan Drain Plugs		11562588
1 Set	Pistons, Flat Top	+ 0.010, +0.030, +0.040	
1 Set	Pistons, Dished Top	+ 0.010, +0.030	
1 Set	Rods		
1 Set	Rod Bearings	0.001, 0.010, Under-sized	CB743A-C
1 Set	Main Bearings	STD, .010, Under-sized	MS2327A-C
1	Rear Main Seal		12587621
1	Oil Filter, GM		
	Truck, Long		PF1218
	Truck, Short		PF454
1	Valley Tray		12559929
1	Crankshaft	4500, Forged	Raylar

Quantity	*Item Name*	*Size/Description*	*Part Number*
1	Reluctors, Fore and Aft, Pair		Raylar
1 Set	Cam Bearings	CHP 12	
1	Rear Cam Plug		3999200
	CYLINDER HEADS		
2	Cylinder Heads (Complete Springs, Locater Base, Retainer, Locks, Studs, Guide Plates)		
2	Pipe Plugs	½" Pipe	
2	Shallow Freeze Plugs	1-⅜" diameter	
1 Set	Head Gaskets, Performance	0.041	
RT and LT	Head Gaskets, Stock	0.060	
36	Head Bolt, 18 Total per Head, Raylar		
28	Head Bolt, 14 per Head, Long	10 × 110	
8	Head Bolt, 4 per Head, Short	10 × 60	
36	Stainless Washer	10 mm	
1 Set	Rocker, Stainless Roller	1.7	Raylar
1 Set	Rocker Nuts, 16 AFN, for Stainless Rocker Arms		Raylar
2	Valve Covers with Coil Boss with Gasket		12591507
2	Valve Covers without Coil Boss		
14	Valve Cover Bolts		12559598
14	Valve Cover Bolt Seal		12557831
2	Valve Cover O-ring Gaskets to Head		12559597
8	Spark Plugs, Delco		
	41-800, Washer		
	41-983 AC, Taper		
	MR43 LTS AC, Taper		
8	Intake Pushrods, Stock	8.180	12556295
	Manton	+.060	
8	Exhaust Pushrods, Stock	9.130	12556296
	Manton	+.060	
8	Guide Plates		12562369
16	Rocker Stud		12569721
	INTAKE MANIFOLD, RAYLAR		
10	Intake Manifold Bolts ARP w/ Washer	6 × 80 mm	
10	Intake Manifold Bolts GM, Black Long	6 × 72 mm	11609264
1	Throttle Body, Raylar Marine	80 or 90 mm	Raylar
1	Throttle Body Gasket		12570168

Quantity	*Item Name*	*Size/Description*	*Part Number*
2	Oil Filler Cap, 2004–2007	A/C Delco FC 208	12573337
1	Oil Filler 2004–2007 Plastic Filler		12581140
1	MAP Sensor, GM	213–796	9359409
1	Intake Air Temperature (IAT) Sensor, GM	213–190	25036751
1	Bolt MAP Retainer	6 × 25 mm	
1	Mercury Marine Idle Air Control (IAC) Motor, Ford		
1	Mercury Marine IAC Motor Gasket, Ford		
1	Mercury Marine IAC Motor Adapter, Mercury		
1	IAC Motor EGR Cover Plate, GM	2004–2006 EGR Block-off plate	
1	IAC Motor EGR Cover Gasket, GM	219–330	12580673
2	Bolt IAC Adapter to Manifold	8 × 30 mm	
2	Bolt IAC to Adapter	6 × 20 mm	
2	Intake Gaskets (GS), Steel and O-ring		
	2001–2004 Early Steel		89017539
	2004–2009 Late Steel		89017343
8	Fuel Injectors, 42 lb GM Industrial 3 Hole		
1 Set	Fuel Rails, Modified		Raylar
1	Fuel Crossover		Raylar
2	Fuel Crossover Lock Clips		Raylar
1	Injector Loom		Raylar
4	Studs, Fuel Rail	6 mm	11518950
4	Nuts, Fuel Rail Studs	6 mm	3530297
	Fuel Pressure Regulator, 8.1L	Adjustable	12574986
	WATER PUMP & MISCELLANEOUS		
2	Gasket Pump to Block Water Gaskets		12592020
4	Bolts Pump to Block	10 mm × 1.5 × 65 mm	11516109
1	Crossover, Mercury		
2	Gasket for Crossover to Head, GM Crossover		12571593
1	Tensioner		12580828
2	Bolts Tensioner	10 mm × 1.5 × 55 mm	
2	Stainless Studs, Mercury	7⁄16 × 3"	
4	Water Crossover Bolts	10 mm × 1.5 × 30 mm	11516328

Resources

Resources & Suppliers

Accel Manufacturing Inc.
www.holley.com/brands/accel
(866) 464-6553

Armstrong Race Engineering (ARE)
www.drysump.com
(916) 652-5282

Arizona Speed and Marine
www.azspeed.com
(480) 753-0208

Automotive Racing Parts (ARP)
www.arp-bolts.com
(800) 826-3045

Banks Power Products
(aka Gale Banks Engineering)
www.bankspowerproducts.com
(888) 623-4373

BBK Performance
www.bbkperformance.com
(386) 624-0025

Borla Performance Industries
www.borla.com
(877) 462-6752

Boostpower USA, Inc.
www.boostpower.com
(805) 498-888

Buddy Bar Casting
www.buddybarcasting.com
(562) 861-9664

Callies
www.callies.com
(419) 435-2711

Cloyes
www.cloyes.com
(479) 646-1662 x 297

CNS Motors
www.cnsmotors.com
(626) 452-1153

COMP Cams
www.compcams.com
(800) 999-0853

Crower Cams
www.crower.com
(619) 661-6477

Crusader Engines
www.crusaderengines.com

Darin Morgan
www.darinmorgan.net

Dart Machinery, Ltd.
www.dartheads.com
(248) 362-1188

Dooley Enterprises
www.dooleyenterprises.com
(714) 630-6436

Edelbrock
www.edelbrock.com
(888) 799-1135

EFI Live
www.efilive.com
+64 (9) 534-1188

FAST Fuel Air Spark Technology
www.fuelairspark.com
(877) 334-8355

F&B Performance Engineered Products
www.fbthrottlebodies.com
(858) 324-1770

Gibson Performance Exhaust
www.gibsonperformance.com
(800) 528-3044

GM Parts Direct
www.gmpartsdirect.com
(336) 760-7046

GM Parts Headquarters
(Genuine OEM Parts)
gmpartsheadquarters.com
(833) 860-4248

Gromm Racing
Hank Slocum
664 Stockton Ave Unit J
San Jose, CA 95126
(408) 287-1301

GT Racing heads
Greg Burkhart
2735 Banner Whitehead Rd
Sophia, NC 27350
(336) 905-7988

Hilborn Fuel Injection
www.hilborninjection.com
(949) 360-0909

Hofman Design
www.hofmandesign.com
(949) 378-4746

Holley
www.holley.com
(866) 464-6553

Indmar Marine Engines
www.indmar.com

JEGS High Performance Parts
www.jegs.com
(800) 345-4545

Jesel
www.jesel.com
(732) 901-1800

IPSCO, LLC
www.ipsco.org
(303) 252-4481

Kinsler Fuel Injection
www.kinsler.com
(248) 362-1145

LS1/8.1 Swap Information
www.lt1swap.com

Marine Power
www.marinepowerusa.com
(877) 388-9555

ME Racing Service
www.meracing.com
+46 (0) 243 100 66

MEFI Burn
www.mefiburn.com
(310) 793 2410

Melling
www.melling.com
(517) 787-8172 x 2527

Mercury Marine
www.mercurymarine.com/en/us
(920) 929-5040

Mercury Racing
www.mercuryracing.com

MSD
www.holley.com/msd
(888) 258-3835

Murph's Speedboat Shop
www.murphsspeedboatshop.com
(619) 746-0256

Nutech Engine Systems
(760) 440-3029

O'Reilly Auto Parts
www.oreillyauto.com
888-327-7153

Pacific Cast Products.
pacificcastproducts.com
(562) 400-2702

Pertronix
www.pertronix.com
(800) 827-3758

Pleasurecraft Engine Group
pleasurecraft.com
(803) 345-1337

Power Solutions International (PSI)
www.psiengines.com
(630) 350.9400

Precision Marine
www.precisionmarine.biz
(480) 986-0969

Procharger
www.procharger.com
(913) 338-2886

Pro-Filer Performance Products
www.profilerperformance.com
(937) 846-1333

Raylar Engineering
www.raylarengineering.com
(866) 496-8181

Reher Morrison Racing Engines
rehermorrison.com
(855) 467-4880

Rinda Technologies
www.rinda.com
(773) 736-6633

Roush Fenway Racing
www.roushperformance.com
(800) 597-6874

S. A. Gear
www.sagearinc.com
(800) 269-0363

S D Engine-Flow-Rite
(619) 220-4981

Seakamp Engineering
www.seakamp.com
(360) 734-2788

Speed Master
www.speedmaster79.com
(909) 605-1123

Stainless Works
www.stainlessworks.net
(800) 878-3635

Summit Racing Equipment
www.summitracing.com
(800) 230-3030

T&D Machine Products
www.tdmach.com
(775) 884-2292

Volvo Marine
www.volvopenta.us

Vortech Superchargers
www.vortechsuperchargers.com
(805) 247-0226

Whipple Superchargers
www.whipplesuperchargers.com
(559) 442-1261

Wholesale Automotive Machine Inc.
www.wamenginesd.com
(619) 281-1400

World Products, Inc.
www.worldproducts.com
(707) 996-5201

Books

Chevy Big-Blocks: How to Build Max Performance on a Budget
David Vizard

GM Performance Parts Catalog

How to Rebuild Small-Block Mopar Engines
by yours truly, Don Taylor and Larry Hofer, published by HP Books